STUDY GUIDE

Discovering Deuteronomy

W. Robert Godfrey

LIGONIER MINISTRIES

Renew your Mind.

LIGONIER.ORG | 800-435-4343

Table of Contents

Introduction   3
Study Schedules   5
The Structure of Deuteronomy   7

1   The Shape of Deuteronomy   8
2   The Author of Deuteronomy   15
3   The History in Deuteronomy (1-4)   22
4   The God of Deuteronomy (5-10:11)   29
5   Blessed above All Peoples (6-7)   36
6   Called to Believe & Obey (8-10)   43
7   Laws about Loving God (10:12-11)   50
8   What Loving God Looks Like   57
9   Living as God's Holy People (13-14)   64
10   Worshiping God   71
11   The Feasts of Israel (16)   78
12   Laws about Leadership (17)   85
13   Laws about Priests (18-19)   92
14   Laws about Loving Your Neighbor (19-20)   99
15   Laws about Conflict (20-21)   106
16   Laws Relating to Purity (22)   113
17   What Loving Your Neighbor Looks Like (23-25)   120
18   Warnings That Protect Us (26-27)   127
19   Warnings That Call Us to Faithfulness (28)   134
20   Warnings That Call Us to Obedience (29-30)   141
21   Deuteronomy Points Us to Christ (31-34)   148

Introduction

Deuteronomy is one of the most frequently quoted Old Testament books in the New Testament. So, why do modern Christians often overlook it? In this twenty-one-part teaching series, Dr. W. Robert Godfrey reveals the importance and value of studying Deuteronomy. Through an examination of the book's structure and context, this series will help students better understand Deuteronomy's coherent message. *Discovering Deuteronomy* connects the history, land, leaders, laws, and warnings of Deuteronomy to the New Testament and to modern life. In doing so, it highlights the relevance and usefulness of this foundational book.

This study guide is a companion to the video teaching series. Whether you are using the DVDs, streaming the videos on Ligonier.org, or going through the course in Ligonier Connect, this resource is designed to help you make the most of the learning experience. For each message in the series, there is a corresponding lesson in this guide. Here is what you will find in each lesson:

INTRODUCTION	The introduction is a brief paragraph that summarizes the content covered in the lecture and considered in the study guide lesson.
	How to use: Use the introduction to each lesson to get a sense of the big picture before watching the video. Refer to these statements as you work through the study guide to remind you of what you have already covered and where you are headed.
LEARNING GOALS	The learning goals are the knowledge and skills the study guide lesson will endeavor to equip you with as you work through the lecture content.
	How to use: Familiarize yourself with the goals of each lesson before engaging its contents. Keeping the overall purpose in mind as you watch each video and reflect on or discuss the questions will help you get the most out of each lesson.
KEY IDEAS	The key ideas are the major points or takeaways from the lecture.
	How to use: Use these ideas to prepare yourself for each lesson and to review previous lessons. They describe specifically the knowledge each lecture is communicating.

REFLECTION & DISCUSSION QUESTIONS	The questions are the guided reflection and/or discussion component of the lesson that are intended to help you prepare for, process, and organize what you are learning. **How to use:** Reflect on individually or discuss in a group the questions in the order in which they appear in the lesson. The timestamps in the right margin indicate where the answers to questions during the video can be found.
PRAYER	The prayer section offers suggestions for how to close the lesson in prayer with respect to what was taught in the lecture. **How to use:** Consider using each lesson's prayer section as a guide to personal or group prayer. These sections follow the ACTS prayer model, which you can learn more about in R.C. Sproul's Crucial Questions booklet *Does Prayer Change Things?* This helpful guide is available as a free e-book at Ligonier.org.
REVIEW QUIZ	The review quiz is a set of six multiple-choice questions that appears at the end of each lesson. **How to use:** Use each quiz to check your comprehension and memory of the major points covered in each lecture. It will be most beneficial to your learning if you take a lesson's quiz either sometime between lessons or just before you begin the next lesson in the study guide.
ANSWER KEY	The answer key provides explanations for the reflection and discussion questions and answers to the multiple-choice questions in the review quiz. **How to use:** Use the answer key to check your own answers or when you do not know the answer. Note: Do not give in too quickly; struggling for a few moments to recall an answer reinforces it in your mind.

Study Schedules

The following table suggests four plans for working through the *Discovering Deuteronomy* video teaching series and this companion study guide. Whether you are going through this series on your own or with a group, these schedules should help you plan your study path.

	Extended 23-Week Plan	Standard 21-Week Plan	Abbreviated 10-Week Plan	Intensive 8-Week Plan
Week	**Lesson**			
1	*	1	1–3	1–3
2	1	2	4 & 5	4–6
3	2	3	6 & 7	7 & 8
4	3	4	8 & 9	9–11
5	4	5	10 & 11	12 & 13
6	5	6	12 & 13	14–16
7	6	7	14 & 15	17 & 18
8	7	8	16 & 17	19–21
9	8	9	18 & 19	
10	9	10	20 & 21	
11	10	11		
12	11	12		
13	12	13		
14	13	14		

Week	Extended 23-Week Plan	Standard 21-Week Plan	Abbreviated 10-Week Plan	Intensive 8-Week Plan
	Lesson			
15	14	15		
16	15	16		
17	16	17		
18	17	18		
19	18	19		
20	19	20		
21	20	21		
22	21			
23	*			

* For these weeks, rather than completing lessons, spend your time discussing and praying about your learning goals for the study (the first week) and the most valuable takeaways from the study (the last week).

The Structure of Deuteronomy

Throughout this teaching series, Dr. Godfrey makes reference to the literary structure of Deuteronomy. Please use the diagram below as a reference point as you work your way through this study guide. This will help you see where the passage you are studying fits into the book of Deuteronomy as a whole.

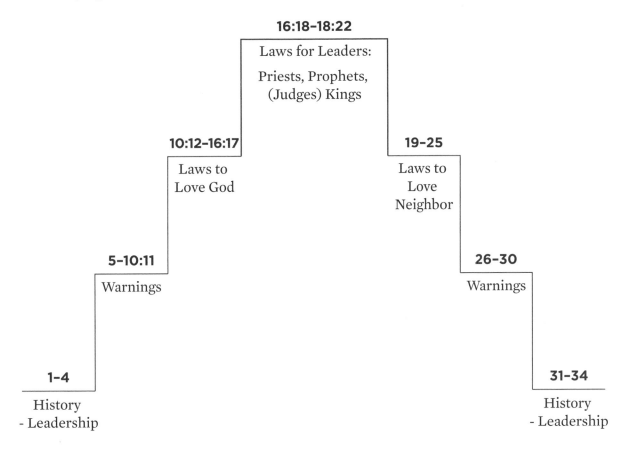

1

The Shape of Deuteronomy

INTRODUCTION

The book of Deuteronomy, though often overlooked, is important for Christians today. In its own right, it contains the law and the history of God's people. In light of the New Testament, it provides continuity from the law of Moses to its fulfillment through Jesus. Closely examining the structure of Deuteronomy will help the meaning become clearer and more relevant.

LEARNING GOALS

When you have finished this lesson, you should be able to:

- Know why it is important to study Deuteronomy
- Understand how the book is structured and why
- Recognize the continuity between the Old Testament and the New Testament

KEY IDEAS

- Deuteronomy speaks to Christians today about a big picture of what the life of God's people ought to be in light of His great saving work for them.
- The history of the Israelites is the history of every Christian.
- By understanding Moses' role, we better understand the role of Jesus.
- Deuteronomy has a distinct structure that explores concepts about history, law, love, and leadership.

REFLECTION & DISCUSSION QUESTIONS

Before the Video

What Do You Think?

Take a moment to answer the following questions. They will prepare you for the lecture.

- Have you studied Deuteronomy before? Why do you think this book is often overlooked?

- What is the structure of a typical story? How does following this general format help with understanding the story?

Scripture Reading

And the Word became flesh and dwelt among us, and we have seen his glory, glory as of the only Son from the Father, full of grace and truth. (John bore witness about him, and cried out, "This was he of whom I said, 'He who comes after me ranks before me, because he was before me.'") For from his fullness we have all received, grace upon grace. For the law was given through Moses; grace and truth came through Jesus Christ.

—John 1:14–17

- How does this passage relate Jesus to Moses?

During the Video

Answer the following questions while you watch the video. They will guide you through the lecture.

Foundations of Deuteronomy   0:00–18:00

- What are some general elements that can be found in the book of Deuteronomy?

- What are some examples of the continuity between the Old and New Testaments?

- What role does Moses play in Deuteronomy and our study of it?

Meaning from Structure   18:00–24:53

- As Dr. Godfrey describes and draws the structure of Deuteronomy, draw it yourself, along with labels.

- How was the book of Deuteronomy originally delivered and why?

After the Video

Answer the following questions after you have finished the lecture. They will help you identify and summarize the major points.

- What are some reasons that Christians today might overlook or dismiss the study of Deuteronomy?

  If you are in a group, have the members discuss how they might persuade a skeptical Christian to study Deuteronomy.

- Summarize the analogy that compares the history of Israel to the history of the America. What was the purpose of this analogy?

  If you are in a group, have the members discuss the idea that Deuteronomy has much to teach us about Jesus Christ. Do Christians naturally equate the study of Deuteronomy and the life of Moses with the study of Jesus? Why or why not?

- Why are you undertaking this study on the book of Deuteronomy? Has this first lesson helped you see the significance of studying Deuteronomy? How so?

  If you are in a group, have the members discuss what they hope to get out of this teaching series.

PRAYER

Commit to prayer what you have learned from God's Word in this lesson.

- Praise Jesus for the grace and truth He brought to fulfill the law.
- Confess any prejudice you've held against studying the Old Testament.
- Thank God for the prophets, priests, and kings who pointed toward the ultimate Prophet, Priest, and King.
- Ask God to open your heart and mind to understand and apply the lessons of Deuteronomy throughout this study.

REVIEW QUIZ

Use these multiple-choice questions to measure what you learned from this lesson.

1. Which of these is a common prejudice Christians have about Deuteronomy?
   a. It is about places and people that no longer exist.
   b. It is just a hodgepodge of strange laws.
   c. No one can prove that it was written by Moses.
   d. It contradicts laws found in other books of the Bible.

2. The lecture refers to three types of God's law distinguished by Reformed theology. Which of these is *not* one of those three categories?
   a. The civil law of God that governed Israel in the land
   b. The ceremonial law that governed Israel's holiness
   c. The moral law of God for all times and for all people
   d. The redemptive law of God that is only available to Jews

3. Which of these best describes the continuity between Israel and the church?
   a. The church replaces Israel.
   b. The church displaces Israel.
   c. The church and Israel share a history but not a purpose.
   d. The church fulfills what God was doing in Israel.

4. The overall structure of Deuteronomy is like a mountain range, with alternating ups and downs.
   a. True
   b. False

5. Which is the best definition of a *chiasm*?
   a. A structure of corresponding ideas
   b. A contradiction in Scripture
   c. An Old Testament practice
   d. A law that has been fulfilled

6. Which of these is the pinnacle of the structure of Deuteronomy?
   a. Dietary laws
   b. Moses
   c. Leadership
   d. Warnings

Answer Key—The Shape of Deuteronomy

Before the Video

What Do You Think?

These are personal questions. The answers should be based on your own knowledge and experience.

Scripture Reading

- How does this passage relate Jesus to Moses?

  The passage seems to contrast Jesus with Moses. Moses brought the law; Jesus brought grace and truth. In this lecture, you will see that one is actually the fulfillment of the other.

During the Video

Foundations of Deuteronomy

- What are some general elements that can be found in the book of Deuteronomy?

  In general, the book of Deuteronomy contains laws, places, people, historical events, warnings, the idea of a nation, discussion of land, points about leadership, and information about the religious practices and beliefs of the people of Israel.

- What are some examples of the continuity between the Old and New Testaments?

  The Old Testament prepared people to understand Jesus when He came. Understanding Jesus' roles as Prophet, Priest, and King depends on a firm sense of what those roles meant in the Old Testament. Old Testament concepts of sin and sacrifice help us appreciate Jesus' sacrifice and forgiveness. There is also a strong continuity between Israel and the church as God's people.

- What role does Moses play in Deuteronomy and our study of it?

  Moses served as a mediator between God and His people. He helps us better understand Jesus, who is the greater Mediator. Through Moses, we can understand Jesus better. While Moses gave the people grace and truth through the law, Jesus brought that grace and truth to fulfillment.

Meaning from Structure

- As Dr. Godfrey describes and draws the structure of Deuteronomy, draw it yourself, along with labels.

  Please reference "The Structure of Deuteronomy" on page 7.

- How was the book of Deuteronomy originally delivered and why?

  Moses delivered it as a sermon of approximately five hours to the Israelites. He was about to die, and he was passing the leadership of Israel to Joshua. This sermon prepared the people for this change in leadership and Israel's future.

After the Video

- What are some reasons that Christians today might overlook or dismiss the study of Deuteronomy?

  Those who don't understand the book's structure might find it to be a confusing hodgepodge of information. People might believe that Jesus has replaced Old Testament law, so there is no longer any relevance to it. Perhaps the cultural setting of Deuteronomy can be difficult to relate to.

- Summarize the analogy that compares the history of Israel to the history of America. What was the purpose of this analogy?

  Dr. Godfrey argued that significant historical events like the Revolutionary War inform Americans of their history. The purpose of this analogy was to relate the importance of studying Deuteronomy because, though some people feel detached from the people, places, and events of Deuteronomy, its history is significant to the people of God today.

- Why are you undertaking this study on the book of Deuteronomy? Has this first lesson helped you see the significance of studying Deuteronomy? How so?

  These are personal questions designed to help you focus on your goals for this study while also processing the scope of this series.

REVIEW QUIZ

Lesson 1

1. **B.**
   Without understanding the background, structure, and culture of Deuteronomy, people often see the book as a random collection of strange laws. However, Dr. Godfrey will show how it "is really about a big picture of what the life of God's people ought to be in light of His great saving work for them."

2. **D.**
   The lecture introduces the concept of the moral, civil, and ceremonial dimensions of the law, all of which still have some relevance and usefulness to us today as God's people.

3. **D.**
   The Old Testament and the New Testament are one continuous story of God's work, which was begun in Israel but fulfilled in the New Testament church. The history of Israel is the history of the church right up to the present day.

4. **B.**

   The overall structure of Deuteronomy is like that of a step pyramid, with the steps on one side reflecting the steps on the opposite side.

5. **A.**

   A chiasm is a literary structure that reflects the shape of the Greek letter chi, which is the form of an X and has a focal point at the center. In a chiasm, the structure of the material draws attention to that which is in the center. Throughout this series, Dr. Godfrey uses a step pyramid to represent the structure of Deuteronomy.

6. **C.**

   The pinnacle of the structure of Deuteronomy is leadership. In a way, the entire sermon of Deuteronomy is about leadership, as Moses is preparing the Israelites for their future in the promised land and the transfer of leadership to Joshua.

2

The Author of Deuteronomy

INTRODUCTION

An accurate knowledge of the life of Moses is crucial to understanding and appreciating the meaning and purpose of Deuteronomy. In this lesson, Dr. Godfrey explores the person behind Deuteronomy, examines the setting of the Israelites as they were on the verge of entering the promised land, and shows how the lessons the Israelites learned apply to Christians today.

LEARNING GOALS

When you have finished this lesson, you should be able to:

- Describe the context of Moses' sermon in Deuteronomy
- Understand the importance of leadership in Deuteronomy
- Relate the lessons of the Israelites to contemporary Christian living

KEY IDEAS

- The Israelites disobeyed God as they prepared to enter the promised land and experienced the consequences of their sin.
- Moses prepared the Israelites for the transfer of leadership that began with Joshua and continued through the history of Israel's leaders.
- Moses was an imperfect leader who was prevented from entering the promised land.

REFLECTION & DISCUSSION QUESTIONS

Before the Video

What Do You Think?

Take a moment to answer the following questions. They will prepare you for the lecture.

- What do you know about the events in the life of Moses?

- What are important elements of a farewell speech?

Scripture Reading

For I do not want you to be unaware, brothers, that our fathers were all under the cloud, and all passed through the sea, and all were baptized into Moses in the cloud and in the sea, and all ate the same spiritual food, and all drank the same spiritual drink. For they drank from the spiritual Rock that followed them, and the Rock was Christ. Nevertheless, with most of them God was not pleased, for they were overthrown in the wilderness. Now these things took place as examples for us, that we might not desire evil as they did. . . . Now these things happened to them as an example, but they were written down for our instruction, on whom the end of the ages has come. Therefore let anyone who thinks that he stands take heed lest he fall.

—1 Corinthians 10:1–6, 11–12

- When he wrote to church in Corinth, how did Paul describe the narrative of Moses and the Israelites in the wilderness?

During the Video

Answer the following questions while you watch the video. They will guide you through the lecture.

Moses the Author   *0:00–12:00*

- How do we know that Moses wrote the book of Deuteronomy?

- What is the background and the purpose of Moses' sermon that became the book of Deuteronomy?

- How does Deuteronomy ensure godly leadership under God's law through the separation of powers?

Moses & the Promised Land   *12:00–25:15*

- Summarize the situation as the Israelites arrived at Kadesh-barnea, where they were to enter the promised land.

- Why did Moses begin his sermon recorded in Deuteronomy by talking about leadership?

- What is the significance of the Israelites' defeating Sihon and Og?

After the Video

Answer the following questions after you have finished the lecture. They will help you identify and summarize the major points.

- Why does the book of Deuteronomy address kings when it would be hundreds of years before Israel had a king?

    If you are in a group, discuss how this aspect of Deuteronomy informs the doctrine of Scripture. How does it speak to Scripture's inspiration, authority, or sufficiency?

- How does death in Deuteronomy correspond to Jesus' death on the cross?

    If you are in a group, have the members discuss any parallels they see between Deuteronomy, the New Testament, and Christian life today.

- What changed between the Israelites' first losing battle with the Amorites and their victory forty years later?

    If you are in a group, read aloud Psalms 135 and 136, which celebrate these victories over Sihon and Og. What might the Israelites have thought or felt about God or themselves as they sang these psalms?

PRAYER

Commit to prayer what you have learned from God's Word in this lesson.

- Praise God for being a God who keeps His promises.
- Confess areas of doubt in your life concerning the promises of God.
- Thank God for the preserved history and warnings that point to Christ.
- Ask God to help you apply the insights from this lesson to your life to glorify Him.

REVIEW QUIZ

Use these multiple-choice questions to measure what you learned from this lesson.

1. What part of Deuteronomy do scholars agree was not written by Moses?
   a. The record of Moses' death
   b. The Ten Commandments
   c. The history of the first battle with the Amorites
   d. Dietary laws

2. What does the word *Deuteronomy* mean?
   a. Law of the land
   b. God's Word recorded
   c. The fifth book
   d. The second law

3. Which of these did Moses stress for leaders of Israel?
   a. Submission to God's Word
   b. Submission to God's law
   c. Submission to God's covenant
   d. All of the above

4. How much time passed between Moses' receiving God's law at Mount Sinai and the Israelites' doubt at the border of the promised land?
   a. Four years
   b. Forty years
   c. Eleven days
   d. Two days

5. What sin prevented Moses from entering the promised land?
   a. He destroyed the first set of stone tablets from God.
   b. He did not honor God as holy before the people.
   c. He doubted that the Israelites could defeat the Amorites.
   d. He hesitated to turn over leadership to Joshua.

6. Moses and the first generation of Israelites died before entering the promised land, but that doesn't mean that they perished everlastingly.
   a. True
   b. False

Answer Key—The Author of Deuteronomy

REFLECTION & DISCUSSION QUESTIONS

Before the Video

What Do You Think?

These are personal questions. The answers should be based on your own knowledge and experience.

Scripture Reading

- When he wrote to church at Corinth, how did Paul describe the narrative of Moses and the Israelites in the wilderness?

  These verses show that Paul viewed the wilderness narrative as real history that revealed Christ. He saw this history of the Israelites as an example and a warning against breaking God's law. It shows that Paul took God's promise, and sin and judgment, very seriously.

During the Video

Moses the Author

- How do we know that Moses wrote the book of Deuteronomy?

  The book begins by stating that Moses was the author. In addition, literary study and archaeology have placed it during the time of Moses. It shows coherence as a book written at one time by one author.

- What is the background and the purpose of Moses' sermon that became the book of Deuteronomy?

  The Israelites were camped east of the Jordan River preparing to cross into the promised land. The sermon was meant to prepare the Israelites for this transition into the promised land and also for the transition of leadership from Moses to Joshua. Moses knew the people well and knew their needs. He wanted to say farewell and make sure they could continue walking as God's people.

- How does Deuteronomy ensure godly leadership under God's law through the separation of powers?

  Moses instructed future kings to make a copy of the law, keep it with them, read it, and follow it. Priests ensured that the law was copied accurately. So, the law was handed down by God, carried out by kings, and checked over by priests.

Moses & the Promised Land

- Summarize the situation as the Israelites arrived at Kadesh-barnea, where they were to enter the promised land.

  They had just traveled eleven days from Mount Sinai, where God gave Moses His law. They had just seen the awesome power of God and the fulfillment of His promise as He worked miracles to free them from slavery in Egypt. However, though they had been promised a land flowing with milk and honey, the Israelites doubted God. They feared entering the land after hearing the spies' report. God then told the Israelites they would not enter the land, but they decided to do so anyway. They fought the Amorites and lost, and then they wandered in the wilderness for forty years until the generation that doubted God's promise died.

- Why did Moses begin his sermon recorded in Deuteronomy by talking about leadership?

  He was emphasizing that this book is about leadership. He wanted the people to know that he was not a fully adequate leader and that he needed help. He explained to them how God would provide leadership for the people.

- What is the significance of the Israelites' defeating Sihon and Og?

  Sihon and Og were Amorite kings. Forty years earlier, in disobedience, the Israelites fought the Amorites and were defeated. Now, as the Israelites fought the Amorites again, God gave Israel the victory. This victory marked entrance into the promised land.

After the Video

- Why does the book of Deuteronomy address kings when it would be hundreds of years before Israel had a king?

  Moses gave this sermon to prepare the Israelites for leadership under God's law as that leadership transferred from Moses to Joshua and beyond. Addressing future kings ensured that God's law would be maintained, followed, and preserved.

- How does death in Deuteronomy correspond to Jesus' death on the cross?

  Deuteronomy confronts us with death and the with seriousness of sin and its consequences. Like Jesus' death on the cross, the death of Moses and of the first generation of Israelites reminds us that God judges sin severely.

- What changed between the Israelites' first losing battle with the Amorites and their victory forty years later?

  The first battle was fought in disobedience and was therefore doomed to fail. After forty years in the wilderness, God's judgment had been carried out. All of the disobedient, doubting adults had died, and now God could hand His people the victory.

REVIEW QUIZ

Lesson 2

1. **A.**

   Moses could not have recorded the event of his own death. Scholars agree that this section at the end of Deuteronomy was added by another author. However, the rest of Deuteronomy was written by Moses, as more and more evidence and study testify.

2. **D.**

   The word Deuteronomy *is Greek for "the second law." It may be named this way because the first four books of Moses are considered as the first giving of the law while Deuteronomy is the second.*

3. **D.**

   Moses emphasized leadership under God, not lifting oneself up above God. Leadership in Israel was not to be lawless or under a king who was a law unto himself. Even the king was to submit to the ultimate authority of God.

4. **C.**

   According to Deuteronomy 1:2, "There are eleven days' journey from Horeb by the way of mount Seir unto Kadesh-barnea." As explained in this lesson, Horeb is Mount Sinai and Kadesh-barnea is where the Lord told the Israelites to enter the promised land.

5. **B.**

   In this lesson, Dr. Godfrey mentioned that God told Moses he couldn't enter the promised land "because you did not hold me holy before the people." This incident probably refers to Numbers 20:1–13, where Moses did not obey exactly what the Lord had commanded him.

6. **A.**

   Dr. Godfrey interpreted their physical death as "a statement to the people of God and to the world and to us that sin has consequences, that sin will be judged, and that the judgment is severe." However, there's no indication that they necessarily perished everlastingly for that sin.

3

The History in Deuteronomy

INTRODUCTION

In this lesson, Dr. Godfrey explains the first step of the pyramid structure of Deuteronomy, which is about history. In examining Deuteronomy 1–4, he focuses on the central idea of idolatry, and how that was a problem for the Israelites and for all of God's people who would follow them.

LEARNING GOALS

When you have finished this lesson, you should be able to:

- Know key events in the history of the Israelites in the wilderness
- Understand God's perspective on the seriousness of idolatry
- Explain why it is important not to add to or take away from God's Word

KEY IDEAS

- The Bible doesn't contain a complete history, but it contains a carefully chosen history.
- God is spirit (John 4:24), and He is to be worshiped in spirit rather than by images.
- Idolatry includes the internal matter of the heart and its posture toward God; it is not merely an external matter.

REFLECTION & DISCUSSION QUESTIONS

Before the Video

What Do You Think?

Take a moment to answer the following questions. They will prepare you for the lecture.

- What do you know about the history of the Israelites in the wilderness and their idolatry?

- What is idolatry? What are modern examples of idolatry?

Scripture Reading

And now, O Israel, listen to the statutes and the rules that I am teaching you, and do them, that you may live, and go in and take possession of the land that the LORD, the God of your fathers, is giving you. You shall not add to the word that I command you, nor take from it, that you may keep the commandments of the LORD your God that I command you. Your eyes have seen what the LORD did at Baal-peor, for the LORD your God destroyed from among you all the men who followed the Baal of Peor. But you who held fast to the LORD your God are all alive today. . . . Only take care, and keep your soul diligently, lest you forget the things that your eyes have seen, and lest they depart from your heart all the days of your life. Make them known to your children and your children's children.

—Deuteronomy 4:1–4, 9

- What were the reasons for the law and for preserving it unchanged through generations?

During the Video

Answer the following questions while you watch the video. They will guide you through the lecture.

Deuteronomy 1-4   *0:00-13:52*

- In what ways was Moses similar to modern historians?

- What happened when the Israelites encountered the Moabites, the Ammonites, and the Amorites?

- What important message about idolatry does God repeat in Deuteronomy 4?

A Focus on Chapter 4   *13:52-24:42*

- Overall, what is Deuteronomy 4 about?

- Why does Moses admonish the Israelites not to add or take away anything from this book?

- What was the general nature of idol worship among the Israelites?

After the Video

Answer the following questions after you have finished the lecture. They will help you identify and summarize the major points.

- What was the great snare of the nations that Israel fell into, and into which we still fall today?

If you are in a group, discuss where you see idolatry at work in the culture today and what makes these modern versions of idolatry so attractive.

- In what ways have churches today moved away from being people of the Word?

If you are in a group, have the members discuss the different characteristics that mark a church that is faithful to the Word of God.

- In light of this lesson, what is the importance of family?

If you are in a group, have the members discuss how a church can care for Christians who do not belong to traditional families (e.g., widows, single adults, college students away from home).

PRAYER

Commit to prayer what you have learned from God's Word in this lesson.

- Praise the Lord for preserving the record of His faithfulness for us.
- Confess any areas of idolatry in your life.
- Thank God for the perfection of His Word that never changes.
- Ask God to help you play a role in passing down faithfulness to future generations.

REVIEW QUIZ

Use these multiple-choice questions to measure what you learned from this lesson.

1. Moses summarized the Israelites' forty-year journey in the wilderness as "years upon years."
    a. True
    b. False

2. Why did the Israelites avoid fighting with the people in Moab and Ammon?
    a. The Israelites did not obey God's command to take their lands.
    b. These people far outnumbered them, so the Israelites were afraid.
    c. The Israelites understood that God would not give them victory.
    d. These people were descendants of Lot, their distant relatives.

3. How was Sihon, king of the Amorites, similar to Pharaoh?
    a. Both attempted to recapture the Israelites after allowing them to leave.
    b. Both had hardened hearts in response to a reasonable request from Moses.
    c. Both insisted that the Israelites bow down to worship their idols.
    d. All of the above

4. What is significant about Moses' burial place?
    a. It was on the same mountain where he first met God.
    b. It was actually in the promised land, though he was told he wouldn't enter.
    c. It was the same place where the Apostle Paul would later be buried.
    d. It was unmarked so it could not become a shrine.

5. What background does the book of Numbers give about Baal-peor?
    a. It's where the Israelites fell into idolatry because they had married unbelievers.
    b. It's where the Israelites destroyed their idols in rejection of Baal.
    c. It's where the Israelites were denied entry because of their unbelief.
    d. It's where the people of Baal-peor tried to add to the law that God gave Moses.

6. What theme is at the heart of the fourth chapter of Deuteronomy?
    a. Family
    b. God's promises
    c. Doctrine
    d. Idolatry

Answer Key—The History in Deuteronomy

REFLECTION & DISCUSSION QUESTIONS

Before the Video

What Do You Think?

These are personal questions. The answers should be based on your own knowledge and experience.

Scripture Reading

- What were the reasons for the law and for preserving it unchanged through generations?

  Obeying these statutes and judgments meant that the Israelites would live in and possess the promised land. Refraining from adding to or deleting from it would ensure that they could obey the law in full. The reason to preserve the law for future generations was so that they would not forget what God has done and what He commands.

During the Video

Deuteronomy 1–4

- In what ways was Moses similar to modern historians?

  Like modern historians, Moses had to choose the most critical events of the past to include in his history. He chose aspects of Israel's history that were relevant to his farewell sermon and to the transition of leadership that would take place.

- What happened when the Israelites encountered the Moabites, the Ammonites, and the Amorites?

  The Israelites avoided the lands of Moab and Ammon because Moses didn't want them to fight their relatives. At the land of the Amorites, Moses asked if the Israelites could pass through peacefully. King Sihon refused, which led to war and a total defeat of the Amorites.

- What important message about idolatry does God repeat in Deuteronomy 4?

  Deuteronomy 4 reminds the Israelites that when God spoke to them at Mount Sinai, He took no form. The theme is that God is spirit, and those who worship Him must do so in spirit and in truth (cf. John 4:24). The Israelites are to be a people of the Word, not of images.

A Focus on Chapter 4

- Overall, what is Deuteronomy 4 about?

Although it is part of the "history" step of the pyramid, it contains a lot of overlapping law and warnings. This chapter is itself a chiasm, with the matter of idolatry at the center.

- Why does Moses admonish the Israelites not to add or take away anything from this book?

  The general truth of God's Word, as echoed in Revelation, is that God has told us everything we need to know. We don't need to add to it because any additions wouldn't be from Him, and we shouldn't take away from it or we'll miss something essential to the Word that He has given. We are simply to know, cherish, and obey the Word because it is sufficient.

- What was the general nature of idol worship among the Israelites?

  In general, they did not reject the Lord outright. Instead, they allowed themselves to be influenced by others, as in the example of intermarriage. They continued to love and serve the Lord, but they also sought to worship and serve Baal and other idols. Their sin was that they didn't give the Lord their undivided love.

After the Video

- What was the great snare of the nations that Israel fell into, and into which we still fall today?

  The great snare of the nations was idolatry, or worshiping false gods. This is not a trivial matter, as God calls His people to faithful worship of Him alone. Throughout the history of the church, God's people have been susceptible to the same snare of worshiping idols instead of the Lord.

- In what ways have churches today moved away from being people of the Word?

  This lesson mentioned the way the Roman Catholic Church has wandered away from the Word to more visual ceremonies and the way liberal Protestants wander toward their own reason and judgment.

- In light of this lesson, what is the importance of family?

  The family is a structure established by God, not by man. It is the means by which faithfulness can be passed from generation to generation. God has called parents to make the truth about God as fully known as possible to their children.

REVIEW QUIZ

Lesson 3

1. **B.**

   Deuteronomy 2:1 states, "Then we turned and journeyed into the wilderness in the direction of the Red Sea, as the Lord told me. And for many days we traveled around Mount Seir." Moses summarizes their forty-year journey as "many days."

2. **D.**

   Moses did not want the Israelites to fight with the descendants of Lot or other distant relatives. That's why they passed through Moab and Ammon.

3. **B.**

   Moses records that the heart of Sihon was hard and obstinate in response to the reasonable request to pass through the land peacefully. Similarly, Pharaoh's heart was hardened when Moses asked if the people could leave to worship God.

4. **D.**

   Moses asked God to let him enter the promised land with his people, but instead, God allowed Moses to climb Mount Nebo and see the promised land from afar. When Moses died, he was buried there in an unmarked grave. This has prevented his final resting place from becoming a shrine for pilgrimage.

5. **A.**

   Deuteronomy 4:3 states that the Lord destroyed those Israelites who followed Baal at Baal-peor. Numbers provides the background that these Israelites had intermarried with unbelievers at Baal-peor, thus falling into idolatry and Baal worship.

6. **D.**

   The theme of Deuteronomy 4 is the sin of idolatry, summarized by the question: "Do you love the Lord with all your heart?" Idolatry is not primarily about not having statues but about the internal posture of the heart toward God.

4

The God of Deuteronomy

INTRODUCTION

In this lesson, Dr. Godfrey transitions from the history of Deuteronomy 4 to the warnings of Deuteronomy 5–10:11 by focusing on God's commands to avoid idolatry and to keep the Sabbath. Dr. Godfrey explains the reasons behind these commands, what they meant for the Israelites, and how they apply to the church.

LEARNING GOALS

When you have finished this lesson, you should be able to:

- Explain God's reasons for prohibiting idols
- Understand why Moses prophesied that Israel would lose the land
- Know God's reasons for commanding us to keep the Sabbath

KEY IDEAS

- Moses warned the Israelites that turning to idolatry would result in their losing the land.
- Exodus 20 and Deuteronomy 5 offer different reasons behind God's command to keep the Sabbath.
- The Christian Sabbath is on Sunday to represent God's new covenant through Christ's resurrection on the first day of the week.

REFLECTION & DISCUSSION QUESTIONS

Before the Video

What Do You Think?

Take a moment to answer the following questions. They will prepare you for the lecture.

- The Ten Commandments are a unique portion of Scripture. What makes them unique, and why do you think God gave them to His people?

- In what ways does culture recognize some form of Sabbath? In what ways does culture not recognize the Sabbath?

Scripture Reading

*Take care, lest you forget the covenant of the L*ORD *your God, which he made with you, and make a carved image, the form of anything that the L*ORD *your God has forbidden you. For the L*ORD *your God is a consuming fire, a jealous God. When you father children and children's children, and have grown old in the land, if you act corruptly by making a carved image in the form of anything, and by doing what is evil in the sight of the L*ORD *your God, so as to provoke him to anger, I call heaven and earth to witness against you today, that you will soon utterly perish from the land that you are going over the Jordan to possess. You will not live long in it, but will be utterly destroyed.*

—Deuteronomy 4:23–26

- What is God's tone in this passage? What would an Israelite who heard this passage for the first time think about the importance of avoiding idolatry?

During the Video

Answer the following questions while you watch the video. They will guide you through the lecture.

Why Idolatry?   0:00–14:50

- What are some reasons God prohibited His people from making idols?

- What prophecy does Moses make in Deuteronomy 4:25–28?

- Why is idolatry tempting?

Deuteronomy 5–10:11   14:50–24:48

- From what different perspectives do these chapters look at warnings?

- How does Deuteronomy 5 approach warnings from the perspective of Sinai?

After the Video

Answer the following questions after you have finished the lecture. They will help you identify and summarize the major points.

- Read Hebrews 12:28–29. Based on passages like this one, did God's command to guard true worship or God's warnings against idolatry lessen in the New Testament? Why?

  If you are in a group, have the members discuss the false ideas people sometimes construct of the "Old Testament God" compared to the "New Testament God." How are these false views of God developed and propagated?

- In Deuteronomy 4:25–28, Moses prophesies that God's people will act corruptly and be exiled from their land. Immediately following, in verses 29–31, God provides the promise that they will return to Him and be forgiven. What do these two passages teach about God's justice, discipline, and mercy?

  If you are in a group, discuss how this same pattern of corruption, consequence, and redemption happens in the life of a Christian.

- What reasons for keeping the Sabbath are mentioned, and where do they come from?

  If you are in a group, discuss different practices that mark Sabbath observance.

PRAYER

Commit to prayer what you have learned from God's Word in this lesson.

- Praise the Lord for being a God who cannot be embodied by earthly idols.
- Confess any idols you have served.
- Thank God for His mercy in forgiving idolaters.
- Ask God for discernment and strength to obey His commands.

REVIEW QUIZ

Use these multiple-choice questions to measure what you learned from this lesson.

1. God forbade His people from making idols because He is a jealous God.
   a. True
   b. False

2. What important message of Deuteronomy 4 is echoed throughout Scripture?
   a. Keep your body pure.
   b. Be careful how you worship.
   c. Moses was punished for disobedience.
   d. The Lord is an angry God who seeks vengeance.

3. What modern spiritual practice does this lecture address as idolatry?
   a. Reading forms for baptism
   b. Taking the Lord's Supper
   c. Praying to the saints
   d. Confessing one's sins

4. What is a possible reason for establishing cities of refuge, as discussed in this lesson?
   a. It showed that sinners must be separated from God's people.
   b. It helped put an end to blood feuds.
   c. It kept non-Israelites from mingling with God's people.
   d. It preserved the ways of the past.

5. Where do the commandments given in Exodus 20 and those given in Deuteronomy 5 differ?
   a. In the stipulations of those protected by the command not to murder
   b. In the inclusion of a command not to covet
   c. In the order of the command to have no idols
   d. In the reason behind the command to keep the Sabbath

6. According to church history, why was the Sabbath moved from Saturday to Sunday?
   a. To allow people to work on Saturdays
   b. To better coincide with church worship services
   c. To emphasize the beginning rather than the end of the week
   d. To mark the new covenant and Christ's resurrection

Answer Key—The God of Deuteronomy

REFLECTION & DISCUSSION QUESTIONS

Before the Video

What Do You Think?

> *These are personal questions. The answers should be based on your own knowledge and experience.*

Scripture Reading

- What is God's tone in this passage? What would an Israelite who heard this passage for the first time think about the importance of avoiding idolatry?

  God's tone is serious, sober, and clear. He obviously cares a great deal about whether His people participate in idolatry, and He provides clear consequences if they do. Israelites who heard this passage for the first time would be struck by the danger of idolatry and the character of their holy God who will not tolerate rival gods among His people.

During the Video

Why Idolatry?

- What are some reasons God prohibited His people from making idols?

  No created thing is an appropriate representation of God. He wants His people to worship the Creator, not the creation. Creating idols diminishes and replaces God. It undermines the personal and loving nature of His relationship with His people.

- What prophecy does Moses make in Deuteronomy 4:25–28?

  Moses correctly predicts that the people of Israel will act corruptly and will, as a result, be exiled from the land.

- Why is idolatry tempting?

  Idolatry can tempt us to think we have something physical to connect us to the divine. It appeals to our visual nature. There are routines, such as praying to saints, that people still wrongly cling to for comfort.

Deuteronomy 5–10:11

- From what different perspectives do these chapters look at warnings?

  Chapters 5, 9, and 10 look at warnings from the perspective of Sinai. Chapter 6 is from the perspective of the family. Chapter 7 is from the perspective of Israel's relationship to the world. Chapter 8 is from the perspective of Israel as a nation.

- How does Deuteronomy 5 approach warnings from the perspective of Sinai?

  Deuteronomy 5 repeats the Ten Commandments, which were handed down from God on Mount Sinai in Exodus 20. The commandments remain the same, but Deuteronomy 5 introduces a new reason behind the fourth commandment, keeping the Sabbath holy. This reiteration focuses on God's redemptive work of delivering the Israelites from slavery and delivering all future believers from slavery to sin.

After the Video

- Read Hebrews 12:28–29. Based on passages like this one, did God's command to guard true worship or God's warnings against idolatry lessen in the New Testament? Why?

  Guarding true worship is just as important, if not more so, in the New Testament as it is in the Old Testament, as Hebrews 12:28–29 teaches. Idolatry remains the perennial temptation for the people of God and must be fought against and repented of by God's people in every generation.

- In Deuteronomy 4:25–28, Moses prophesies that God's people will act corruptly and be exiled from their land. Immediately following, in verses 29–31, God provides the promise that they will return to God and be forgiven. What do these two passages teach about God justice, discipline, and mercy?

  These passages speak of an unfortunate cycle for God's people in a fallen world. They will continue to sin, receive God's discipline for sin, and then repent and know His merciful forgiveness. For the Christian, this cycle of repentance and faith is the process of sanctification.

- What reasons are discussed for keeping the Sabbath, and where do they come from?

  Exodus 20 provides the pattern of creation as a reason for resting on the seventh day. God's work of six days of creation and one day of rest is the reason that Christians also work for six days and then rest for a full day. Deuteronomy 5 establishes God's redemptive work as a reason to observe the Sabbath. Because God delivered us from slavery, we have been given rest. A one-day-in-seven Sabbath rest reminded the Israelites of both creation and redemption.

REVIEW QUIZ

Lesson 4

1. **A.**

   Deuteronomy 4:23–24, as quoted in the lecture, says, "Take care, lest you forget the covenant of the LORD your God, which he made with you, and make a carved image, the form of anything that the LORD your God has forbidden you. For the LORD your God is a consuming fire, a jealous God."

2. **B.**

   The message of Deuteronomy 4 is to be careful how you worship. Moses warns the Israelites to take care that they don't forget God's covenant and make a carved image. The discussion of idols emphasizes the idea that God must be worshiped with reverence and awe, as repeated in Hebrews 12.

3. **C.**

   This lesson addressed praying to the saints as a form of idolatry. There is no indication that the forms read in the Dutch Reformed churches are a type of idol, nor are baptism, taking part in the Lord's Supper, or confessing sins.

4. **B.**

   Cities of refuge helped put an end to generations-long blood feuds. Those who committed murder, either intentionally or accidentally, could be sent away yet still be protected from revenge.

5. **D.**

   While the commands are the same, the reason for keeping the Sabbath differ. Exodus 20 focuses on God's work of creation. Deuteronomy 5 focuses on God's redemptive work in delivering His people from slavery.

6. **D.**

   While Saturday is considered the last day of the week and Sunday the first, the shift was not about weekly position of these days but the new covenant of Christ. Christ rose from the dead on the first day of the week. John calls this "the Lord's day" in Revelation 1:10.

5

Blessed above All Peoples

INTRODUCTION

Deuteronomy 6–7 delivers warnings to the Israelites as individuals and as families. In this lesson, Dr. Godfrey will examine the warnings contained in this section and how to apply them. Dr. Godfrey will explain the reasoning and the heart behind these warnings, which are not to punish or restrict us but are a part of God's blessing to us.

LEARNING GOALS

When you have finished this lesson, you should be able to:

- Understand how the warnings of Deuteronomy are tightly linked to the history of Israel
- Recognize the purpose behind God's commands
- Know the warnings God gave the Israelites concerning other nations

KEY IDEAS

- God intends to bless His people, giving them cause for joy and thanksgiving.
- God wants His people to keep His laws on their hearts because doing so shows love and fear of God.
- God wants His people to guard against allowing other nations to draw them away from Him and His laws.

REFLECTION & DISCUSSION QUESTIONS

Before the Video

What Do You Think?

Take a moment to answer the following questions. They will prepare you for the lecture.

- How do you view God when you think of His commands and warnings?

- What rules and warnings do parents give to their children? What is their reasoning behind them?

Scripture Reading

When your son asks you in time to come, "What is the meaning of the testimonies and the statutes and the rules that the LORD our God has commanded you?" then you shall say to your son, "We were Pharaoh's slaves in Egypt. And the LORD brought us out of Egypt with a mighty hand. And the LORD showed signs and wonders, great and grievous, against Egypt and against Pharaoh and all his household, before our eyes. And he brought us out from there, that he might bring us in and give us the land that he swore to give to our fathers. And the LORD commanded us to do all these statutes, to fear the LORD our God, for our good always, that he might preserve us alive, as we are this day. And it will be righteousness for us, if we are careful to do all this commandment before the LORD our God, as he has commanded us."

—Deuteronomy 6:20–25

- How does obedience to commands relate to righteousness?

During the Video

Answer the following questions while you watch the video. They will guide you through the lecture.

Obedience in the Family   *0:00–13:55*

- How does the *Shema* in Deuteronomy 6:4 echo the Ten Commandments given in Deuteronomy 5?

- Why does Deuteronomy 6 include history as well as commands?

- Why do we have God's commands? Why do we keep them?

Obedience among the Nations   *13:55–25:01*

- What was God's instruction to the Israelites as His chosen people about their interactions with other nations?

- What is God's specific warning about idols in Deuteronomy 7? What is the reasoning behind it?

After the Video

Answer the following questions after you have finished the lecture. They will help you identify and summarize the major points.

- Deuteronomy 6:6 says, "And these words that I command you today shall be on your heart." What does it mean for something to be "on your heart"? What does it not mean?

If you are in a group, have the members discuss the Scripture verses that they have memorized and hidden in their hearts.

- What are some of the rituals from this lesson that people observe in an attempt to keep God's Word on their hearts?

If you are in a group, share some possible rituals or routines for keeping God's Word on the heart. How can Christians keep spiritual disciplines from becoming thoughtless routines?

- In what ways do God's laws and warnings protect and bless the Christian? In what ways does disobedience lead to negative consequences?

If you are in a group, have the members discuss how Christians can speak positively and gratefully about God's laws and warnings to a new Christian or to a skeptic.

PRAYER

Commit to prayer what you have learned from God's Word in this lesson.

- Praise God for His promise to bless you.
- Confess any resentment you've had toward God's commands.
- Thank God that you are declared righteous through Jesus and His perfect obedience.
- Ask God to help you show your love for Him through obedience to His commands.

REVIEW QUIZ

Use these multiple-choice questions to measure what you learned from this lesson.

1. What is the *Shema*?
   a. The Jewish act of atonement for sin
   b. Punishment for breaking a commandment
   c. Israel's confession that the Lord is one
   d. A prayer for protection against enemies

2. When Moses tells the people to remember Massah, to what event is he referring?
   a. Receiving water from a rock in the wilderness
   b. Defeating an enemy who far outnumbered the Israelites
   c. Witnessing God Himself in the form of a cloud
   d. The ground's swallowing up a man who disobeyed God

3. Moses taught that the main reason to keep God's laws is to become righteous.
   a. True
   b. False

4. To what does Moses compare idolatry and intermarriage with other nations?
   a. A plague
   b. A flame
   c. A snare
   d. A famine

5. At the center of this section, what is at the heart of all these warnings?
   a. The Israelites have a chance to start anew in the promised land.
   b. God's people are like sheep gone astray.
   c. God wants to bless His people.
   d. No one can be righteous without the law.

6. Why did God drive the nations out of the land and give it to the Israelites?
   a. They were turning the Israelites away from the Lord.
   b. They would not repent of their sinfulness.
   c. They were not the ones chosen by the Lord.
   d. They had dishonored the Lord in the way they used the land.

Answer Key—Blessed above All Peoples

REFLECTION & DISCUSSION QUESTIONS

Before the Video

What Do You Think?

These are personal questions. The answers should be based on your own knowledge and experience.

Scripture Reading

- How does obedience to commands relate to righteousness?

  This passage might make it sound as if righteousness comes from obedience. However, this lesson will explore the truth that obeying commands is simply an outward sign of love for and fear of God.

During the Video

Obedience in the Family

- How does the *Shema* in Deuteronomy 6:4 echo the Ten Commandments given in Deuteronomy 5?

  The Shema *states that the Lord is one God and that He is the only God of Israel. It is a confession that there are no other gods. He is singular and exclusive. Similarly, the first and second commandments establish God as the God of Israel, with no other gods before Him.*

- Why does Deuteronomy 6 include history as well as commands?

  In this section about remembering the laws, Moses tells the Israelites to remember also that God gave them the land. By remembering God's faithfulness, they protect their own faith and keep from doubting whether God is really with them. They can pass on these stories to their children as evidence of God's faithfulness.

- Why do we have God's commands? Why do we keep them?

  God's laws grow out of the history of God's people. According to this lesson, the Israelites have the laws because God delivered them from Egypt and brought them to the promised land. We obey God's commands because it is good for us to do so. It shows fear of the Lord.

Obedience among the Nations

- What was God's instruction to the Israelites as God's chosen people about their interactions with other nations?

  They were to avoid the snare of idolatry and intermarriage. They were set apart to be holy for their own benefit and blessing. They had nothing to fear from the nations because God is powerful to accomplish His purposes. These lessons still apply to Christians today.

- What is God's specific warning about idols in Deuteronomy 7? What is the reasoning behind it?

  God commanded the Israelites to destroy completely the idols of the nations they were going to dispossess. He knew that the Israelites would be tempted to salvage the silver and gold that covered the idols and turn these precious metals into other objects. But God knew that these can become idols in their own right. He wanted those things to be set aside for destruction and His people to be set aside for holiness.

After the Video

- Deuteronomy 6:6 says, "And these words that I command you today shall be on your heart." What does it mean for something to be "on your heart"? What does it not mean?

  Having "these words" on your heart doesn't mean just reading them or even memorizing them and then moving on. Moses goes on to explain that they should be taught to children, talked about throughout the day, and even written down as signs on the doorposts of the home. Fundamentally, this communicates that "these words" are to encompass all of our lives.

- What are some rituals from this lesson that people observe in an attempt to keep God's Word on their heart?

  Orthodox Jews wear a small box on their foreheads with a written portion of the law in it. They have a similar container on the lintel of their door, which they touch when entering or leaving the home. Many Christians pray when waking, at bedtime, and at mealtimes. In old Dutch Reformed homes, families also read the Bible and prayed after meals.

- In what ways do God's laws and warnings protect and bless the Christian? In what ways does disobedience lead to negative consequences?

  God's laws and warnings express the character of God, define the threat of sin, describe the consequences of disobedience, and instruct God's people in how they should live. God is faithful to discipline His people if they refuse to follow His laws and heed His warnings. Discipline is never pleasant (Heb. 12:11), but it is a sign of God's love.

REVIEW QUIZ

Lesson 5

1. **C.**

   Shema *is the Hebrew word for "hear." It is a call and a warning to acknowledge the Lord as one. The* Shema *states, "Hear, O Israel: the LORD our God, the LORD is one."*

2. **A.**

   In the wilderness at Massah, the Israelites thought they were dying of thirst. They questioned Moses and questioned whether God was really with them. They wondered if God had brought them out into the desert just to die of thirst. In response, God had Moses strike a rock, which then poured forth water for them to drink.

3. **B.**

   Deuteronomy 6:25 states, "And it will be righteousness for us, if we are careful to do all this commandment before the Lord our God." Moses does not mean that we become righteous because we obey the law. Rather, we obey the law because we love and fear God, who gives us righteousness as a gift by grace alone through faith alone in Christ alone (Eph. 2:8–10).

4. **C.**

   Moses refers to idolatry and intermarriage with other nations as a snare. It is a trap that lures us and then boxes us in. The Lord warns Israel to be careful and alert by comparing idolatry to a snare.

5. **C.**

   At the center of this section, God calls His people to be careful because He intends to bless them above all peoples. God's intention is to bless them, leading them to rejoice and give thanks to Him for His goodness.

6. **B.**

   God drove the nations out of the land because they did not repent of their sinfulness. God would not have driven them away just to give the land to the Israelites, because that would be unjust.

6

Called to Believe & Obey

INTRODUCTION

In this lesson, Dr. Godfrey examines the warnings to the nation of Israel in Deuteronomy 8–10, demonstrating the strong ties between the message of the Old Testament and that of the New Testament, and how those are applied in the church. Building on previous lectures, Dr. Godfrey will continue to explore themes of leadership, idolatry, and blessing.

LEARNING GOALS

When you have finished this lesson, you should be able to:

- Know how Jesus' temptation in the wilderness parallels the Israelites' temptations in the wilderness
- Understand how God's works in the past are a motivation for thanksgiving
- Balance belief with obedience and balance God's mercy with His holiness

KEY IDEAS

- God, who provides for all our needs, warns us not to take credit for His blessings.
- Obedience is a result of belief, and both are important in following God.
- God blesses those who keep His covenant and punishes those who don't.

REFLECTION & DISCUSSION QUESTIONS

Before the Video

What Do You Think?

Take a moment to answer the following questions. They will prepare you for the lecture.

- Can you recall the details of Jesus' temptation in the wilderness?

- Do you see faith and works as two opposing influences, as two sides of the same coin, or as something else?

Scripture Reading

*Take care lest you forget the L*ORD *your God by not keeping his commandments and his rules and his statutes, which I command you today, lest . . . you forget the L*ORD *your God, who brought you out of the land of Egypt, out of the house of slavery . . . who fed you in the wilderness with manna that your fathers did not know, that he might humble you and test you, to do you good in the end. Beware lest you say in your heart, "My power and the might of my hand have gotten me this wealth." You shall remember the L*ORD *your God, for it is he who gives you power to get wealth, that he may confirm his covenant that he swore to your fathers, as it is this day. And if you forget the L*ORD *your God and go after other gods and serve them and worship them, I solemnly warn you today that you shall surely perish. Like the nations that the L*ORD *makes to perish before you, so shall you perish, because you would not obey the voice of the L*ORD *your God.*

—Deuteronomy 8:11, 14, 16–20

- In this passage, what reasons are listed for God's blessings on Israel?

During the Video

Answer the following questions while you watch the video. They will guide you through the lecture.

Deuteronomy & Jesus   *0:00–7:15*

- What are some of the connections between Deuteronomy 8 and Jesus' temptation in the wilderness?

Belief & Obedience   *7:15–24:10*

- What should the attitude of the Israelites be after God gives them the land?

- What is the relationship between belief and obedience?

After the Video

Answer the following questions after you have finished the lecture. They will help you identify and summarize the major points.

- What's the difference between God's providing manna in the wilderness and Jesus' turning stones to bread in the wilderness?

  If you are in a group, have the members discuss how Jesus' resistance to temptation should be an encouragement to Christians.

- Read Psalm 78. Identify the three areas of temptation that both the Israelites and Jesus faced.

  If you are in a group, discuss what form these temptations take today.

- What is the prosperity gospel? How is the prosperity gospel opposed to what God has actually promised?

  If you are in a group, have the members discuss modern examples of prosperity gospel preaching or thinking.

PRAYER

Commit to prayer what you have learned from God's Word in this lesson.

- Praise God for sending a Son who knows what it is to be tempted.
- Confess times that you have given in to temptation.
- Thank God that He is both holy and merciful.
- Ask God for the discernment to balance His warnings and threats with His promises and provision.

REVIEW QUIZ

Use these multiple-choice questions to measure what you learned from this lesson.

1. Complete Deuteronomy 8:3. "And he humbled you and let you hunger and fed you with manna, which you did not know, nor did your fathers know, that he might make you know that . . ."
    a. ". . . his chosen leader is Moses."
    b. ". . . the Lord your God preserved you."
    c. ". . . the Lord keeps his covenant."
    d. ". . . man does not live by bread alone."

2. Which of Jesus' directives is most similar to the message of Deuteronomy 8?
   a. "Do not be anxious about your life, what you will eat or what you will drink, nor about your body, what you will put on" (Matt. 6:25).
   b. "You shall love your neighbor as yourself" (Matt. 22:39).
   c. "Go therefore and make disciples of all nations . . . teaching them to observe all that I have commanded you" (Matt. 28:19–20).
   d. "If you would be perfect, go, sell what you possess and give to the poor" (Matt. 19:21).

3. The disobedience of the Israelites in making the golden calf was egregious because God had told them to destroy the gold they used to make the calf.
   a. True
   b. False

4. Which of these was *not* an outcome of the incident with the golden calf?
   a. Moses offered his life to spare the Israelites.
   b. The calf was ground into powder and scattered.
   c. The Lord forgave the people of Israel.
   d. Aaron turned over his position to his son Eliezer.

5. What is the one great truth that summarizes Deuteronomy 5–10:11?
   a. God will bless those who keep His covenant and punish those who don't.
   b. Anyone who practices idolatry will be cut off from the land God promised.
   c. When we face temptation, God will always provide a way out of that temptation.
   d. God has provided a path for continual leadership among His people.

6. What are the two sides of the tightrope that Christians must walk so that we don't fall too far to either side?
   a. God's mercy and God's holiness
   b. The Old Testament and the New Testament
   c. Our own spiritual growth and the evangelism of others
   d. Belief in God and remembering the past

Answer Key—Called to Believe & Obey

REFLECTION & DISCUSSION QUESTIONS

Before the Video

What Do You Think?

> *These are personal questions. The answers should be based on your own knowledge and experience.*

Scripture Reading

- In this passage, what reasons are listed for God's blessings on Israel?

    The passage says that God blessed Israel (by bringing them out of slavery and providing manna) to humble and test them to do them good. He blessed them (with the promised land) to fulfill the covenant He swore to their fathers.

During the Video

Deuteronomy & Jesus

- What are some of the connections between Deuteronomy 8 and Jesus' temptation in the wilderness?

    The connections between Deuteronomy 8 and Jesus' temptation are that Jesus quotes Deuteronomy 8:3 at His first temptation; Jesus' forty days of fasting remind us of the Israelites' forty years in the wilderness; Jesus is the new Israel and the new Moses; Jesus and the Israelites faced hunger and thirst; the devil tempts Jesus with bread because God gave His people manna; both Jesus and the Israelites are tempted about food, power, and worship; Jesus depends on God rather than taking matters into His own hands, which is the lesson the Israelites should have learned in the wilderness.

Belief & Obedience

- What should the attitude of the Israelites be after God gives them the land?

    They are not to act as if they were given the land because of their own righteousness. Instead, it is because of the wickedness of the nations that God drove them out. The Lord did it to confirm the covenant He made with Abraham, Isaac, and Jacob. It is not a reward for their goodness or obedience. "He is rescuing a stubborn people. He is not rewarding a righteous people."

- What is the relationship between belief and obedience?

    One cannot exist without the other. When Moses said to the Israelites that they neither believed nor obeyed, he is connecting belief and obedience intimately together. We are therefore called to believe, and out of that belief to obey. Obedience becomes the fruit of believing.

After the Video

- What's the difference between God's providing manna in the wilderness and Jesus' turning stones to bread in the wilderness?

   The provision of manna in the wilderness built dependence on God. The Israelites could only collect enough for one day and then trust that more would appear the next day. It was not through the power and might of their own hands. In contrast, the devil tempted Jesus to take matters into His own hands by providing His own bread.

- Read Psalm 78. Identify the three areas of temptation that both the Israelites and Jesus faced.

   Both faced temptation in the areas of food (v. 18), power (v. 42), and worship (v. 58).

- What is the prosperity gospel? How is the prosperity gospel in opposition to what God has actually promised?

   The prosperity gospel says, "If you really follow the Lord, He'll make you healthy and wealthy." While God blesses those who love and obey Him, we have no guarantee that those blessings will come in the form of health and wealth. The greatest blessings the Lord gives are spiritual blessings.

REVIEW QUIZ

Lesson 6

1. **D.**

   The full text of Deuteronomy 8:3 is this: "And he humbled you and let you hunger and fed you with manna, which you did not know, nor did your fathers know, that he might make you know that man does not live by bread alone, but man lives by every word that comes from the mouth of the LORD."

2. **C.**

   In the Great Commission, Jesus tells His disciples to teach the nations to observe all that He had commanded. Similarly, the message of Deuteronomy 8 is that "man lives by every word that comes from the mouth of the LORD." Both are a call to obey God's commands.

3. **B.**

   According to the lesson, the worst part about this betrayal was that the Israelites named the golden calf Yahweh. They didn't just turn to another god; they also gave God's holy name to their man-made idol.

4. **D.**

   All of these except for the last option resulted from the incident of the golden calf. Eliezer took over as priest for Aaron only after Aaron died.

5. **A.**

   The lesson stated this truth in this way: "I will bless you as you keep My covenant, and I will punish you as you fail to keep My covenant."

6. **A.**

   While all of these options require some degree of balance, this lesson specifically referenced God's mercy and God's holiness. Leaning too far to the side of mercy ignores God's justice. Leaning too far to the side of holiness ignores God's forgiveness.

7

Laws about Loving God

INTRODUCTION

The third section of the pyramid-like structure of Deuteronomy is laws about loving God. In this lesson, Dr. Godfrey explores how God's laws are for the benefit and blessing of His people and how loving God applies to life in the church by tying together themes of keeping God's Word on our hearts, being careful, and remembering what God has done for us.

LEARNING GOALS

When you have finished this lesson, you should be able to:

- Understand how loving God involves loving your neighbors
- Value God's work in history and in the church and teach it to your children
- Know how to grow in daily dependence on God for His blessings

KEY IDEAS

- God's laws and commandments are for the good of His people and should produce a loving relationship with God and with neighbors.
- God's history must be preserved by passing it on to the next generation.
- God's blessings build our daily trust and dependence on Him.

REFLECTION & DISCUSSION QUESTIONS

Before the Video

What Do You Think?

Take a moment to answer the following questions. They will prepare you for the lecture.

- In what ways do you show love for God?

- What events in Old Testament history have taught you the most about God's character?

Scripture Reading

*And now, Israel, what does the L*ORD *your God require of you, but to fear the L*ORD *your God, to walk in all his ways, to love him, to serve the L*ORD *your God with all your heart and with all your soul, and to keep the commandments and statutes of the L*ORD*, which I am commanding you today for your good? Behold, to the L*ORD *your God belong heaven and the heaven of heavens, the earth with all that is in it. Yet the L*ORD *set his heart in love on your fathers and chose their offspring after them, you above all peoples, as you are this day.*

—Deuteronomy 10:12–15

- What does this text reveal as the significance of God's choosing Israel as His people?

During the Video

Answer the following questions while you watch the video. They will guide you through the lecture.

Deuteronomy 10   0:00–10:04

- What are the three parts of the Heidelberg Catechism? How do they relate to Deuteronomy 10?

- How do warnings and commandments correspond to loving God and neighbor?

- What historical example is given of the church's growth because of God's blessing?

Deuteronomy 11   10:04–23:14

- What is the importance of Korah's story referenced in Deuteronomy 11?

- What was the point of the illustration of farming with irrigation as opposed to farming with rainfall?

After the Video

Answer the following questions after you have finished the lecture. They will help you identify and summarize the major points.

- Why is it necessary for man's love for God to spill over and create love for neighbors and sojourners as well?

If you are in a group, discuss how you have seen Christians show love for neighbors and strangers.

- Why is biblical history important?

If you are in a group, have the members discuss the importance of learning biblical history and how Christians can grow in their knowledge of biblical history in the context of a church.

- What examples does Deuteronomy provide of how God's people learned to depend on Him daily for blessings?

If you are in a group, have the members discuss the different types of circumstances that God uses teach Christians to depend on Him daily. Be sure to include both positive and negative circumstances.

PRAYER

Commit to prayer what you have learned from God's Word in this lesson.

- Praise God for being worthy of our love and obedience.
- Confess the ways that you have failed to love others as God loves you.
- Thank God for His daily blessings that reveal His faithfulness.
- Ask God to show you how you can love Him more.

REVIEW QUIZ

Use these multiple-choice questions to measure what you learned from this lesson.

1. According to this lesson, which of these is the intention of God's law?
   a. A standard against which we can measure our behavior
   b. A personal connection between God and man
   c. A safety net to protect against harmful behaviors
   d. A response to the disobedience of the Israelites

2. Which of these is an example of compassion in the law of Moses?
   a. Murderers are not put to death.
   b. Those who steal are not put to death.
   c. Sojourners are to be given a stipend.
   d. Widows are to be taken in by priests.

3. The Israelites went down to Egypt as seventy people, and they left Egypt as millions.
   a. True
   b. False

4. Which of these was used to illustrate the importance of remembering history?
   a. The golden calf
   b. The sin of Korah
   c. Twentieth-century China
   d. All of the above

5. How does Deuteronomy 11 contrast Egypt and Israel?
   a. Individuals vs. community
   b. Slaves vs. conquerors
   c. Irrigation vs. rain
   d. Hunting vs. herding

6. What important point does Moses repeat in Deuteronomy 11?
   a. Moses will not enter the promised land.
   b. God's people are not to create idols.
   c. God's people are to keep God's Word on their hearts.
   d. God provided manna in the wilderness.

Answer Key—Laws about Loving God

REFLECTION & DISCUSSION QUESTIONS

Before the Video

What Do You Think?

These are personal questions. The answers should be based on your own knowledge and experience.

Scripture Reading

- What does this text reveal as the significance of God's choosing Israel as His people?

  In this passage, Moses restates what is required of Israel before God, and it is Israel's great privilege to be His people because out of all the nations of the earth, God chose them even though "heaven and the heaven of heavens, the earth with all that is in it" belong to Him.

During the Video

Deuteronomy 10

- What are the three parts of the Heidelberg Catechism? How do they relate to Deuteronomy 10?

  Part 1 deals with guilt or sin, part 2 deals with grace, and part 3 deals with gratitude. They relate to Deuteronomy 10 because we sin when we break God's commandments. This puts us in constant need of God's grace and deliverance from sin. Because God so lovingly lavishes this grace on us, we always have reason for gratitude.

- How do warnings and commandments correspond to loving God and neighbor?

  Love and humanity are embedded in the law of Moses and result in our building a loving community. Those who love God want to obey His commands. That love spills over into the community, resulting in love for family, neighbors, and sojourners. It is what separates God's people as light in a dark world.

- What historical example is given of the church's growth because of God's blessing?

  In the twentieth century, the church in China remained small and struggled to grow, even after a century or more of work by missionaries. Once Communist leaders threw out the missionaries and banned the church, it grew dramatically.

Deuteronomy 11

- What is the importance of Korah's story referenced in Deuteronomy 11?

  It is an example of remembering God's history by passing it down to younger generations. There will be those who did not live to see these events, so they must be taught of God's triumphs and judgments. It's important because it shows that Korah was so reviled that his name wasn't mentioned, but also so well known that it needed no mention.

- What was the point of the illustration of farming with irrigation as opposed to farming with rainfall?

  When God moved His people from Egypt to Israel, they went from farming that used irrigation, which was by the work of their own hands, to greater dependence on rain, which would be through God's blessing because He could send rain to bless them or withhold it if they were unfaithful.

After the Video

- Why is it necessary for man's love for God to spill over and create love for neighbors and sojourners as well?

  God commands us to love our neighbors and sojourners, as in Deuteronomy 10:18–19: "He executes justice for the fatherless and the widow, and loves the sojourner, giving him food and clothing. Love the sojourner, therefore, for you were sojourners in the land of Egypt." We are to follow God's example of love, which He gave to us even when we did not deserve it.

- Why is biblical history important?

  It teaches us God's faithfulness through His triumphs and His judgments. There are parts of the Bible that assume the audience is knowledgeable about the history of God and His people.

- What examples does Deuteronomy provide of how God's people learned to depend on Him daily for blessings?

  In the wilderness, they depended on God daily to provide manna and quail. They could not provide or store up for themselves any more than what God provided each day. In the promised land, they had no way to irrigate their crops. They had to depend on God daily for rain.

REVIEW QUIZ

Lesson 7

1. **B.**
   While an argument can be made for any of the options as an application of God's law, the lesson teaches that the true intention behind the law is to create personal connection between God and man.

2. **B.**

   In the Mosaic law, those who steal are to be punished but not put to death. Murderers are to be put to death. Sojourners and widows are to be loved, clothed, and fed. However, there is nothing in the law about giving widows a stipend or priests' taking them in.

3. **A.**

   Deuteronomy 10:22 states, "Your fathers went down to Egypt seventy persons, and now the LORD your God has made you as numerous as the stars of heaven."

4. **D.**

   All of these helped illustrate the point that history should be remembered. The golden calf and the sin of Korah dealt with biblical history and have spiritual importance. The example of twentieth-century China served as a reminder to us today that it is ultimately God who builds His church.

5. **C.**

   Deuteronomy 11:10–11 states: "For the land that you are entering to take possession of it is not like the land of Egypt, from which you have come, where you sowed your seed and irrigated it, like a garden of vegetables. But the land that you are going over to possess is a land of hills and valleys, which drinks water by the rain from heaven."

6. **C.**

   Deuteronomy 11:18 is a very close repetition of 6:6–9, in which Moses commands the Israelites to keep God's Word on their hearts.

8

What Loving God Looks Like

INTRODUCTION

From God's first directives to the Israelites to the teaching of Jesus Christ, Scripture reveals that worship is the primary way we love God. In this lesson, Dr. Godfrey studies Israel's fundamental calling to be worshipers of the one true God through studying the commands and warnings in Deuteronomy and focusing on Jesus' teaching and the proper attitude toward worship.

LEARNING GOALS

When you have finished this lesson, you should be able to:

- Know how God directed His people to worship Him
- Understand the posture of both God and man toward worship
- Explain how Jesus defined the nature of true worship

KEY IDEAS

- God gave His people specific directives about how to worship Him and how not to worship Him.
- Worship should be God's people rejoicing in the relationship they have with God.
- Because of Jesus, Christians worship God in spirit and truth in the heavenly Jerusalem.

REFLECTION & DISCUSSION QUESTIONS

Before the Video

What Do You Think?

Take a moment to answer the following questions. They will prepare you for the lecture.

- How would you describe what it is to love God to someone who asked what loving God looks like?

- How did Jesus worship God?

Scripture Reading

The woman said to him, "Sir, I perceive that you are a prophet. Our fathers worshiped on this mountain, but you say that in Jerusalem is the place where people ought to worship." Jesus said to her, "Woman, believe me, the hour is coming when neither on this mountain nor in Jerusalem will you worship the Father. You worship what you do not know; we worship what we know, for salvation is from the Jews. But the hour is coming, and is now here, when the true worshipers will worship the Father in spirit and truth, for the Father is seeking such people to worship him."

—John 4:19–23

- What kind of people does God seek?

During the Video

Answer the following questions while you watch the video. They will guide you through the lecture.

The Heart of Worship   *0:00–15:32*

- What is the significance of God's directing the Israelites to worship Him in Jerusalem?

- What is God's attitude toward worship?

- What should our attitude toward worship be?

Perspectives on Worship   *15:32–25:12*

- What role did the Levites play in worship?

- How does Jesus speak about worship in His conversation with the Samaritan woman?

After the Video

Answer the following questions after you have finished the lecture. They will help you identify and summarize the major points.

- How does Dr. Godfrey suggest responding to someone who says there are contradictions in the Bible?

  If you are in a group, have the members discuss how to talk about this topic with a skeptic.

- Describe what worship looks like in churches today.

  If you are in a group, discuss which parts of the worship of God are necessary for true Christian worship.

- How did worship unite the Israelites? How does it unite Christians today?

  If you are in a group, pick three different continents and discuss how Christian worship may look in churches on each continent. What should encourage Christians about the unity in worship they have with other Christians around the world?

PRAYER

Commit to prayer what you have learned from God's Word in this lesson.

- Praise God for calling us to worship Him.
- Confess the ways that you have neglected worship.
- Thank God that we worship Him in the reality of the new Jerusalem.
- Ask God to help you build unity in your church.

REVIEW QUIZ

Use these multiple-choice questions to measure what you learned from this lesson.

1. What is the one place God directs the Israelites in Deuteronomy to go to worship Him?
   a. The tabernacle
   b. Their own homes
   c. The wilderness
   d. Jerusalem

2. God commanded the Israelites not to inquire about pagan gods under any circumstances.
   a. True
   b. False

3. How does the story of Jephthah from the book of Judges relate to the lesson of Deuteronomy 12?
   a. He tore down the high places of pagan worship.
   b. He found the book of the law and reinstated worship.
   c. He offered to sacrifice his own daughter to God.
   d. He encouraged the people to worship false gods.

4. How did God use worship to build community among the Israelites?
   a. By giving them different musical gifts that worked together
   b. By giving all of them different roles in working at the temple
   c. By commanding them to give a tithe to the Levites
   d. By reminding them not to go off to solitary places

5. What does God repeatedly command the Israelites not to eat?
   a. The blood of an animal
   b. Animals that have been sacrificed
   c. Animals that have a mutation
   d. The choicest parts of the fat

6. What theological question does it seem the Samaritan woman is asking Jesus?
   a. Are you the Messiah?
   b. Who was the greatest prophet?
   c. Are the Samaritans or the Jews right?
   d. How can Samaritans be saved?

Answer Key—What Loving God Looks Like

REFLECTION & DISCUSSION QUESTIONS

Before the Video

What Do You Think?

> *These are personal questions. The answers should be based on your own knowledge and experience.*

Scripture Reading

- What kind of people does God seek?

  Jesus' teaching here reveals, as this lesson will further explore, that God ultimately seeks to make true worshipers, those who worship Him in sprit and truth.

During the Video

The Heart of Worship

- What is the significance of God's directing the Israelites to worship Him in Jerusalem?

  It shows that God is prophesying the future, because He already knows this place will exist and that He will be worshiped there. It witnesses to the cohesion of the Bible and what we know of God's character. It sets apart their worship from pagan worship and ensures that pagan places of worship are not repurposed.

- What is God's attitude toward worship?

  We are to worship God His way. He is serious about the way we relate to Him through worship. God does not want His followers going outside the boundaries He has set for worship, and He especially doesn't want them adopting pagan practices.

- What should our attitude toward worship be?

  Rejoicing should be at the heart of our worship. Worship should be the joy of our heart rather than a duty to check off our list. We should not do what is right in our own eyes but do what God requires of us, even when it is difficult. Our worship of God should influence the way we structure and plan our whole lives.

Perspectives on Worship

- What role did the Levites play in worship?

  They received the tithe from the other tribes. They supported the temple by serving as priests and supporting worship.

- How does Jesus speak about worship in His conversation with the Samaritan woman?

  First, he answers her question by confirming that worship should take place in Jerusalem. He then explains that this will change when God seeks those who worship Him in spirit and in truth.

After the Video

- How does Dr. Godfrey suggest responding to someone who says there are contradictions in the Bible?

  The first step is to ask the person to name one of the supposed contradictions. The next is to ask how much of the Bible they've actually read. His point is that the more familiar we become with the Bible, the more cohesion we see.

- Describe what worship looks like in churches today?

  Answers may vary based on experience, but may include music, singing, reading Scripture, taking part in the Lord's Supper, praying, teaching, and giving.

- How did worship unite the Israelites? How does it unite Christians today?

  The Israelites were united by a central place of worship in Jerusalem and the command to return there three times a year. They were also united through the community of dependence that arose from their tithes supporting the Levites. Today, Christians are united because they worship in spirit and truth. Although Christians are in different locations at different times, they worship in the heavenly Jerusalem.

REVIEW QUIZ

Lesson 8

1. **D.**
   Although they had probably not yet heard of Jerusalem, God was directing them there to worship Him. That is where they would build the temple. It's where God would dwell.

2. **B.**
   In Deuteronomy 12:30, God commands the Israelites not to inquire about pagan gods for the purpose of imitating their worship.

3. **C.**
   In the tradition of the pagans, Jephthah was willing to vow to sacrifice his daughter if God would reward him. This example is given to warn the Israelites against how easy it can be to adopt pagan practices.

4. **C.**

   God commanded the Israelites, as a way of worshiping Him, to give a tithe to the Levites. The Levites worked to support the temple. They relied on the other tribes to bring their tithes, and the other tribes relied on them for spiritual leadership.

5. **A.**

   God repeatedly commands the Israelites not to eat the blood of an animal. The blood represented the life of the animal, and God's warning was a way of teaching them to be careful to treasure life.

6. **C.**

   Although Jesus and the Samaritan women discuss such topics as the identity of the Messiah and salvation, the question she seems to be asking Jesus is whether the Samaritans were right to worship outside of Jerusalem.

9

Living as God's Holy People

INTRODUCTION

Many people consider some of the laws in Deuteronomy to be strange, but every law in the book points to something deeper about who God called Israel to be. In this lesson, Dr. Godfrey explains the purpose and symbolism behind some of the seemingly strange laws in Deuteronomy, reinforcing the biblical truths that we are God's children who have been set apart by Him to be holy.

LEARNING GOALS

When you have finished this lesson, you should be able to:

- Know the marks of true and false prophets
- Identify the characteristics of a child of God
- Understand the purpose of Old Testament dietary laws

KEY IDEAS

- God warns His people repeatedly to avoid idolatry by discerning between true and false prophets.
- God gave the Israelites particular laws as a sign that they were a people set apart by Him to be holy.

REFLECTION & DISCUSSION QUESTIONS

Before the Video

What Do You Think?

Take a moment to answer the following questions. They will prepare you for the lecture.

- Why are false prophets, those who wrongly claim to speak for God, so dangerous?

- How are Christians today set apart from non-Christians?

Scripture Reading

You are the sons of the LORD your God. You shall not cut yourselves or make any baldness on your foreheads for the dead. For you are a people holy to the LORD your God, and the LORD has chosen you to be a people for his treasured possession, out of all the peoples who are on the face of the earth.

—Deuteronomy 14:1–2

- Why are God's people called to be holy?

During the Video

Answer the following questions while you watch the video. They will guide you through the lecture.

Deuteronomy 13   *0:00–13:30*

- What are the tests of true and false prophets in this section of Deuteronomy?

- According to Moses' warnings, who might lead the Israelites astray?

- How does the book of Judges relate back to Deuteronomy 13?

Deuteronomy 14   *13:30–24:20*

- What self-awareness does Moses teach God's people to have as they approach worship?

- What is the purpose of God's dietary laws described in the Old Testament?

After the Video

Answer the following questions after you have finished the lecture. They will help you identify and summarize the major points.

- How do false prophets and family members and friends differ in the way they attempt to lead God's people astray?

    If you are in a group, discuss how Christians can identify influences in their lives, personal or cultural, that might subtly be leading them toward idolatry.

- Who are the false prophets of today's culture?

    If you are in a group, discuss the ways that individuals and churches can resist false prophecy and false prophets.

- What was the purpose of the illustration of Baroness Rothschild's actions at the royal palace?

    If you are in a group, discuss different examples of when a Christian in our culture may have to stand up for their Christian faith.

PRAYER

Commit to prayer what you have learned from God's Word in this lesson.

- Praise God for making you His child, set apart to be holy.
- Confess any ways you have entertained false teaching or idolatry.
- Thank God that He fulfilled the law through Jesus Christ.
- Ask God to help you live and worship Him as holy.

REVIEW QUIZ

Use these multiple-choice questions to measure what you learned from this lesson.

1. What type of warning does Moses issue to begin this section of Deuteronomy?
    a. Breaking the Sabbath
    b. Being led astray in worship
    c. Creating false idols
    d. Building high places

2. What does Moses command the Israelites to do about a relative who tries to lead them into idolatry?
    a. Send the person off in exile
    b. Try to steer the person back to God
    c. Report the person to the head priest
    d. Put the person to death

3. Whose birth in Gibeah was made possible because Benjamin disobediently refused to destroy the city?
   a. Saul
   b. David
   c. Moses
   d. Samuel

4. The commandment "You shall not cut yourselves or make any baldness on your foreheads for the dead" refers to pagan mourning practices.
   a. True
   b. False

5. How did Baroness Rothschild risk offending the Queen of England?
   a. She insisted on praying before the meal.
   b. She would not eat food that wasn't kosher.
   c. She asked the queen to cover her head during the meal.
   d. She would not meet with the queen on the Sabbath.

6. Why was Peter ultimately not subject to Old Testament dietary laws?
   a. He had a vision indicating that all animals were clean to eat.
   b. He would need to be around gentiles in his ministry.
   c. The dietary laws had fulfilled their purpose.
   d. Peter was not Jewish.

Answer Key—Living as God's Holy People

REFLECTION & DISCUSSION QUESTIONS

Before the Video

What Do You Think?

> *These are personal questions. The answers should be based on your own knowledge and experience.*

Scripture Reading

- Why are God's people called to be holy?

    This passage explains that God requires His people to be holy precisely because they are His people. They are to be holy as He is holy. They have been chosen as His treasured possession to be His children, and as His children, they are to resemble Him.

During the Video

Deuteronomy 13

- What are the tests of true and false prophets described in this section of Deuteronomy?

    One sign of a true prophet is that what he says comes to pass. Another sign is that he is able to perform miracles. The beauty of these laws about discerning between true and false prophets is that even if one were to perform miracles or prophesy in the manner of a true prophet, he is exposed as a false prophet if he leads God's people into idolatry.

- According to Moses' warnings, who might lead the Israelites astray?

    Throughout this section of Deuteronomy, Moses addresses the harm and temptation to idolatry that might come from false prophets, dreamers, relatives, friends, and "worthless fellows" (Deut. 13:13).

- How does the book of Judges relate back to Deuteronomy 13?

    Deuteronomy 13 warns Israel to completely destroy anyone who tries to lead them astray. Judges 19–20 tell of how Benjamin did not completely destroy Gibeah, and so Saul was born there and became a disobedient king, providing a lesson to Israel.

Deuteronomy 14

- What self-awareness does Moses teach God's people to have as they approach worship?

    God's people should realize that they are a holy people, chosen and set apart by God.

They should also realize that they are children of God and that He is their Father.

- What is the purpose of God's dietary laws described in the Old Testament?

  It is another way for God's people to be set apart. They do not live, worship, or eat like the nations. It also keeps their mind on God throughout the day as they have to consider His commands every time they eat.

After the Video

- How do false prophets and family members and friends differ in the way they attempt to lead God's people astray?

  According to Deuteronomy 13, relatives and close friends approach in secret. They exploit their most intimate relationships. In contrast, false prophets are public figures who attempt to influence as many people as they can at a time.

- Who are the false prophets of today's culture?

  Answers may vary based on experience but can include any cultural influences— speakers, preachers, leaders, authors, groups, or gurus—that lead people astray or promote false teachings about God.

- What was the purpose of the illustration of Baroness Rothschild's actions at the royal palace?

  By refusing to eat any non-kosher food, the Baroness was firmly establishing her obedience to God as more important than her reverence for the queen. The purpose of this illustration was not to uphold the dietary laws of Deuteronomy but to underscore their purpose. By refusing to eat particular foods before the queen, she was in effect saying, "I have been set apart," which was God's intention behind these laws that have been fulfilled in Christ.

REVIEW QUIZ

Lesson 9

1. **B.**
   While these are all forms of idolatry in a sense, Moses specifically warns against being led astray in worship. Deuteronomy 13:1–3 states, "If a prophet or a dreamer of dreams arises among you and gives you a sign or a wonder, and the sign or wonder that he tells you comes to pass, and if he says, 'Let us go after other gods,' which you have not known, 'and let us serve them,' you shall not listen to the words of that prophet or that dreamer of dreams."

2. **D.**
   Unlike the false prophet who seeks to deceive people publicly, Moses warns the Israelites that even their friends and family can tempt them into idolatry by coming to them in secret with destructive teaching. In such a case, the law called for their death (Deut. 13:6–11).

3. **A.**

   Judges 19–20 tell how Israel told Benjamin to wipe out Gibeah completely, but Benjamin disobeyed. As a result, Saul was later born in Gibeah of Benjamin, and the Israelites suffered under him as a disobedient king.

4. **A.**

   This is yet another example of God's warning His people not to follow the worship practices of the pagans, who would cut themselves or shave part of their heads as a sign of mourning.

5. **B.**

   Even at risk of offending the queen of England, this first Jewish guest to have a meal at the royal palace insisted on eating only kosher foods. It was an outward sign that she was set apart and given specific commands by God.

6. **C.**

   While options A and B are both true, the ultimate reason behind Peter's being freed from Old Testament dietary laws is that they had fulfilled their purpose. They were an external sign of God's people being set apart and holy, a people who are now marked by faith in Jesus Christ.

10

Worshiping God

INTRODUCTION

All of God's warnings, commands, and promises reveal the heart of God for His people. In this lesson, Dr. Godfrey further explores the topic of worship by examining some of God's dietary laws and His commands regarding possessions. Dr. Godfrey will show the echoes of Deuteronomy in the New Testament and in modern Judaism.

LEARNING GOALS

When you have finished this lesson, you should be able to:

- Understand the reason behind some of the Old Testament dietary laws
- Know what God commanded in the Old Testament regarding tithes, debts, and slaves
- Recognize how the central message of these Old Testament laws applies to Christians

KEY IDEAS

- God's commands set His people apart as holy and keep Him as the focus of all they do.
- Obeying God's command to give back a portion teaches us to fear the Lord.
- God's underlying desire for us is to show care and compassion for one another.

REFLECTION & DISCUSSION QUESTIONS

Before the Video

What Do You Think?

Take a moment to answer the following questions. They will prepare you for the lecture.

- What might be some habits or rituals that Christians perform that are not directly prescribed in Scripture?

- How have you found biblical generosity to be joyful?

Scripture Reading

*But there will be no poor among you; for the L*ORD *will bless you in the land that the L*ORD *your God is giving you for an inheritance to possess—if only you will strictly obey the voice of the L*ORD *your God, being careful to do all this commandment that I command you today. For the L*ORD *your God will bless you, as he promised you, and you shall lend to many nations, but you shall not borrow, and you shall rule over many nations, but they shall not rule over you.*

—Deuteronomy 15:4–6

- What is the theme of the promises in this passage?

During the Video

Answer the following questions while you watch the video. They will guide you through the lecture.

Worshiping God with Food   *0:00–9:22*

- What has been the outcome of God's command not to boil a young goat in its mother's milk?

- What are some possible explanations for God's command not to boil a young goat in its mother's milk?

Worshiping God with Possessions   *9:22–25:03*

- How does the commandment to tithe teach the fear of the Lord?

- What are God's commands regarding debt and slaves?

After the Video

Answer the following questions after you have finished the lecture. They will help you identify and summarize the major points.

- In what ways have people overinterpreted God's commands in order to be careful?

If you are in a group, discuss any ways you see the overinterpretation of God's commands happening in modern Christian culture.

- How does Jesus reinforce the principles relating to possessions in Deuteronomy 15?

If you are in a group, discuss the ways individual Christians and churches show care and compassion for the poor.

- How do you worship God with your food and with your possessions?

If you are in a group, discuss how you can retain a focus on God in the areas of food and possessions.

PRAYER

Commit to prayer what you have learned from God's Word in this lesson.

- Praise God for His promises of blessing.
- Confess any lack of compassion you have toward others.
- Thank God for the privilege of being a steward of His blessings.
- Ask God to show you ways in which you can better care for the poor.

REVIEW QUIZ

Use these multiple-choice questions to measure what you learned from this lesson.

1. Why did God command the Israelites not to eat an animal that died naturally?
   a. Because they had not observed ritual slaughter
   b. Because the animal was likely unhealthy
   c. As another way of setting them apart
   d. As a way to provide meat for sojourners

2. In discussing biblical "food tests," this lesson mentioned all *except* which of these?
   a. Daniel's refusing the king's rich foods
   b. Jesus' being tempted in the wilderness
   c. Adam and Eve in the garden of Eden
   d. The dietary laws given to the Israelites

3. What biblical lesson is chiefly behind the command to tithe?
   a. Repent of your sins.
   b. Support the priests.
   c. Fear the Lord.
   d. Be generous to others.

4. If an Israelite lived too far from Jerusalem, he could send his tithe with other travelers.
   a. True
   b. False

5. What is the promised outcome of obeying God with our possessions?
   a. Other nations will loan you money.
   b. There will be no poor among you.
   c. You will have no need for slaves.
   d. You will have peace with your neighbors.

6. What is the central message of the commands about debt and slaves?
   a. Be careful to leave an inheritance for your children.
   b. You are superior to other nations.
   c. Be honest in your business dealings.
   d. Show care and compassion for your brothers.

Answer Key—Worshiping God

REFLECTION & DISCUSSION QUESTIONS

Before the Video

What Do You Think?

> These are personal questions. The answers should be based on your own knowledge and experience.

Scripture Reading

- What is the theme of the promises in this passage?

> The theme of this passage is the promise of Israel's prosperity. Some of the most striking features of these promises are that there would not be anyone poor among the nation and that the nation itself would be wealthy without any other nation ruling over it.

During the Video

Worshiping God with Food

- What has been the outcome of God's command not to boil a young goat in its mother's milk?

> In an effort to carefully follow this command, Orthodox Jews completely separate meat and dairy. They keep separate kitchens and cookware for the two, and they wait a certain amount of time between eating the two.

- What are some possible explanations for God's command not to boil a young goat in its mother's milk?

> It's possible that this was a pagan funeral practice, and God didn't want His people to live like the pagans. This explanation would provide parallels with the beginning of Deuteronomy 14. It's also possible that God didn't want His people mixing life with death, as the mother's milk represented life and the young goat represented death. Overall, it is a call to be a holy people set apart from the practices of the nations.

Worshiping God with Possessions

- How does the commandment to tithe teach the fear of the Lord?

> The tithe reminds us that everything we have is from the Lord, received through His blessings rather than through the work of our own hands. Just as dietary laws put God at the center of the lives of the Israelites, the tithe puts God at the center of our

work and finances. It also allows God's people to obey His commands to support the church and to care for the poor.

- What are God's commands regarding debt and slaves?

  Deuteronomy 15 states that an Israelite might have to be enslaved if he can't pay his debts. However, every seven years, debts have to be canceled and Israelite slaves have to be freed. God also warns the Israelites not to take advantage of a poor fellow countryman when he is released. Another law states that a slave can choose to remain a slave after seven years because of his master's generosity. The overall principle of these laws is care and compassion for fellow Israelites.

After the Video

- In what ways have people overinterpreted God's commands in order to be careful?

  Some examples from this lesson: Jews have extrapolated the command to not boil a young goat in its mother's milk to completely avoid any mixing of meat and dairy. In the first century, a common punishment was thirty-nine lashes. Although forty was allowed in the Mosaic law, this punishment of thirty-nine lashes protected against miscounting that would have led to people going beyond the law's limit.

- How does Jesus reinforce the principles relating to possessions in Deuteronomy 15?

  Jesus echoes Deuteronomy 15:11 when He says, "You always have the poor with you" (Mark 14:7). In a way, He is challenging His disciples in their obedience to Deuteronomy 15 because if they had followed God's commands there would be no poor in the land.

- How do you worship God with your food and with your possessions?

  This is a personal question. The answer should take into consideration ways in which the lessons of the laws of Israel can be applied to the Christian life and should reflect ways you practically honor God.

REVIEW QUIZ

Lesson 10

1. **C.**
   God's dietary laws for Israel set them apart from other nations. These commands similarly established them as a people with separate practices. While they were free to give the meat to a sojourner, that was not the purpose behind the command.

2. **A.**
   In his analysis of food tests in the Bible, Dr. Godfrey discusses the dietary laws given to the Israelites, the command that Adam and Eve not eat from the Tree of Knowledge of Good and Evil, and Jesus' temptation in the wilderness to turn stones to bread.

3. **C.**

   Deuteronomy 14:23 clearly states that the chief purpose of the tithe is "that you may learn to fear the LORD your God always." However, it did also go to support priests and it does teach generosity.

4. **B.**

   God made a provision for Israelites who lived far from Jerusalem to exchange their tithe goods for money. These Israelites could travel a long distance more easily with money than with crops and livestock. Once in Jerusalem, the traveling Israelites were to exchange their money for goods and bring those as a tithe.

5. **B.**

   Deuteronomy 15:4–5 contains this promise: "But there will be no poor among you; for the LORD will bless you in the land that the LORD your God is giving you for an inheritance to possess—if only you will strictly obey the voice of the LORD your God, being careful to do all this commandment that I command you today."

6. **D.**

   The central message of these commands is to show care and compassion for fellow Israelites. Debts are eventually to be forgiven, and slaves are regularly to be freed.

11

The Feasts of Israel

INTRODUCTION

Deuteronomy 16 is divided into two sections. In this lesson, Dr. Godfrey examines them to show their application to the Christian life. The first section considers the feasts of Israel, their history, and their purpose. The second section contains more laws about leadership that emphasize earlier themes of being a people set apart and free from idolatry.

LEARNING GOALS

When you have finished this lesson, you should be able to:

- Know the main feasts of the Hebrew calendar
- Relate elements of these feasts to Christianity
- Understand the purpose of judges in Israel

KEY IDEAS

- The three great feasts were important to Israel's past and present.
- Some aspects of Christian worship involve elements of Hebrew feasts.
- God desires a holy people set apart and devoted to Him alone.

REFLECTION & DISCUSSION QUESTIONS

Before the Video

What Do You Think?

Take a moment to answer the following questions. They will prepare you for the lecture.

- What special days or holidays do some Christians celebrate, and what does each attempt to represent?

- Have you ever observed a Jewish festival, such as Passover?

Scripture Reading

Observe the month of Abib and keep the Passover to the Lord your God, for in the month of Abib the Lord your God brought you out of Egypt by night. And you shall offer the Passover sacrifice to the Lord your God, from the flock or the herd, at the place that the Lord will choose, to make his name dwell there. You shall eat no leavened bread with it. Seven days you shall eat it with unleavened bread, the bread of affliction—for you came out of the land of Egypt in haste—that all the days of your life you may remember the day when you came out of the land of Egypt.

—Deuteronomy 16:1–3

- What similarities does this passage have with some of the larger themes in Deuteronomy examined in previous lessons?

During the Video

Answer the following questions while you watch the video. They will guide you through the lecture.

The Great Festivals   *0:00–15:26*

- What are the three great festivals of Israel, and what is the focus of each?

- How does the symbolism of the Passover relate to Christianity?

- How did the Feast of Booths differ from the Day of Atonement?

Local Leadership   *15:26–24:33*

- What kind of leadership does Moses describe beginning in Deuteronomy 16?

- How does the recurring theme of idolatry come up again in this section?

After the Video

Answer the following questions after you have finished the lecture. They will help you identify and summarize the major points.

- How does Dr. Godfrey make sense of the seemingly contradictory commands in Deuteronomy 16: "And you shall rejoice before the Lord your God. . . . You shall remember that you were a slave"?

If you are in a group, discuss how a Christian's remembering his slavery to sin before his conversion can bring him joy in his Christian life.

- What was the benefit of requiring Israelites to travel to Jerusalem for these great feasts?

If you are in a group, discuss the benefit of gathering with like-minded Christians for worship or instruction outside of normal corporate worship (for example, at conferences, meetings, and Christian colleges).

- How did local leadership in the form of judges benefit Israel?

If you are in a group, discuss how biblical church leadership protects and encourages the growth of churches.

PRAYER

Commit to prayer what you have learned from God's Word in this lesson.

- Praise God for being a God of grace, mercy, and provision.
- Confess the times you have not been thankful for God's provision.
- Thank God for delivering you from your past and for providing for your present.
- Ask God to help you act justly in your community.

REVIEW QUIZ

Use these multiple-choice questions to measure what you learned from this lesson.

1. The Feast of the Passover, the Feast of Weeks, and the Feast of Booths are considered the great feasts because they are the longest in duration.
   a. True
   b. False

2. Which feast was also known as the Feast of Pentecost?
   a. Feast of Atonement
   b. Feast of Unleavened Bread
   c. Feast of Booths
   d. Feast of Weeks

3. Which feast was also known as the Feast of Ingathering?
   a. Feast of Tabernacles
   b. Feast of Deliverance
   c. Feast of Firstfruits
   d. Feast of Passover

4. Which of these is *not* mentioned in the lecture as a form of worship during a feast?
   a. Singing
   b. Giving money
   c. Playing instruments
   d. Making sacrifices

5. According to this lesson, the structure of the book of Deuteronomy can also be seen in which of these?
   a. The book of Genesis
   b. The Lord's Prayer
   c. The Westminster Catechism of Faith
   d. The Ten Commandments

6. Why, according to Deuteronomy, does God hate pillars or even a tree near His altar?
   a. They represent Baal, the god of rain.
   b. They represent man's efforts to reach God.
   c. They represent Asherah, the goddess of fertility.
   d. They represent perfection, which man cannot achieve.

Answer Key—The Feasts of Israel

REFLECTION & DISCUSSION QUESTIONS

Before the Video

What Do You Think?

> *These are personal questions. The answers should be based on your own knowledge and experience.*

Scripture Reading

- What similarities does this passage have with some of the larger themes in Deuteronomy examined in previous lessons?

  This passage deals with the history of the Israelites, specifically their deliverance from slavery in Egypt. It is a law or command, and it has to do with what to eat. It centers on the place the Lord will choose and make His name dwell, which is Jerusalem.

During the Video

The Great Festivals

- What are the three great festivals of Israel, and what is the focus of each?

  The Feast of the Passover reminded the Israelites that God brought them out of Egypt. It recalled His grace, mercy, and provision. The Feast of Weeks ties together themes of remembrance and joy. It taught the Israelites to give joyfully to God, who gives them all things. The Feast of Booths reminded the Israelites to rejoice in God's provision because at one time they did not have a land.

- How does the symbolism of the Passover relate to Christianity?

  The unleavened bread reminded the Israelites that they were enslaved and afflicted. Christians know that Jesus delivers us from slavery and affliction. The Israelites celebrated Passover in Jerusalem, where Christ was crucified. They offered a sacrificial lamb, just as Jesus was sacrificed to make atonement for the sins of His people.

- How did the Feast of Booths differ from the Day of Atonement?

  The Day of Atonement did not require going to Jerusalem. It was a solemn day of mourning and fasting. In contrast, the Feast of Booths required going to Jerusalem. It was a time of coming together, feasting, and rejoicing.

Local Leadership

- What kind of leadership does Moses describe beginning in Deuteronomy 16?

  He begins by describing leadership at the local level. Instead of having laws be enforced from the top by a king, the Israelites were to have judges in each town. The judges were to be fair and impartial. These were local leaders who knew their communities well. The system supported the idea of community, fairness, and justice.

- How does the recurring theme of idolatry come up again in this section?

  In the discussion of local judges, there was an admonition against idolatry. A local leader who knows the community is better able to investigate and act on any such practices than a king.

After the Video

- How does Dr. Godfrey make sense of the seemingly contradictory commands in Deuteronomy 16: "And you shall rejoice before the LORD your God. . . . You shall remember that you were a slave"?

  This verse ties together the themes of remembrance and joy. By remembering their slavery, the Israelites remember that they derived no benefit from their own labor. They could rejoice in the freedom that the fruit of their labor belonged to them. In that joy, they were to present the firstfruits to the Lord.

- What was the benefit of requiring the Israelites to travel to Jerusalem for these great feasts?

  Requiring the Israelites to travel to Jerusalem three times a year for the feasts built unity and mutual recognition of the greatness of the Lord. It created a sense of identity and mutual encouragement in seeking the Lord.

- How did local leadership in the form of judges benefit the Israelites?

  In a practical sense, it allowed them to pursue justice because they had a judge at the local level instead of a king who could never hear every case. In a more abstract sense, it helped build community, reminding the Israelites that they were brothers and sisters who could seek fairness before a judge who knew them.

REVIEW QUIZ

Lesson 11

1. **B.**
   The Feast of the Passover, the Feast of Weeks, and the Feast of Booths are considered the great feasts because they carried the requirement of going to Jerusalem to celebrate.

2. **D.**
   The Feast of Pentecost is also known as the Feast of Weeks, the Feast of the Harvest, and the Feast of Firstfruits.

3. **A.**

   The Feast of Ingathering is also known as the Feast of Booths, the Feast of Tabernacles, the Feast of Sheds, and the Feast of Tents.

4. **B.**

   Although this lesson mentioned bringing firstfruits to God as a form of worship, it does not specifically mention giving money.

5. **D.**

   The structure of Deuteronomy echoes the structure of the Ten Commandments. Commandments 1–4 are about loving God, the fifth commandment is about leadership, and commandments 6–10 are about loving one's neighbor. The Westminster Larger Catechism was mentioned as expounding on the fifth commandment as it applies the commandment to leadership in a general sense.

6. **C.**

   An Asherah pole was a pillar dedicated to the pagan goddess of fertility. It was a form of idolatry to erect one, so the Lord hated it.

12

Laws about Leadership

INTRODUCTION

This lesson moves to the pinnacle of the step pyramid that Dr. Godfrey has been using to illustrate the outline of Deuteronomy. In looking at laws about leadership beyond the local level, Dr. Godfrey provides insights into the role and requirements of Israelite kings. The overarching theme of this lesson on leadership is that Jesus is the ultimate Prophet, Priest, King, and Judge.

LEARNING GOALS

When you have finished this lesson, you should be able to:

- Know the Mosaic leadership laws regarding appeals
- Understand that Jesus fulfills the leadership offices established in Deuteronomy
- Understand the reasons behind God's laws for kings

KEY IDEAS

- In addition to local judges, the Israelites had a system of appeals to judges and priests.
- Though God permitted Israel to have a king, Jesus would ultimately fulfill the offices of Prophet, Priest, King, and Judge.
- God set down laws for kings to maintain His purposes for the nation of Israel.

REFLECTION & DISCUSSION QUESTIONS

Before the Video

What Do You Think?

Take a moment to answer the following questions. They will prepare you for the lecture.

- When you hear the term *monarchy*, what ideas come to mind?

- Name some biblical kings with whom you are familiar. Did they have a positive or negative reign?

Scripture Reading

When you come to the land that the LORD your God is giving you, and you possess it and dwell in it and then say, "I will set a king over me, like all the nations that are around me," you may indeed set a king over you whom the LORD your God will choose. . . . And when he sits on the throne of his kingdom, he shall write for himself in a book a copy of this law, approved by the Levitical priests. And it shall be with him, and he shall read in it all the days of his life, that he may learn to fear the LORD his God by keeping all the words of this law and these statutes, and doing them.

—Deuteronomy 17:14–15, 18–19

- What did the Lord require of kings of Israel?

During the Video

Answer the following questions while you watch the video. They will guide you through the lecture.

Fulfillment in Jesus   *0:00–10:18*

- How do the laws in Deuteronomy 17 differ from those in Deuteronomy 16, which were the focus of the previous lesson?

- What roles outlined in Deuteronomy 17 are ultimately fulfilled in Jesus?

Kings & Priests   *10:18–24:39*

- What were God's laws regarding kings?

- What were God's laws regarding priests?

After the Video

Answer the following questions after you have finished the lecture. They will help you identify and summarize the major points.

- In Psalm 89, God promised David that his sons would always sit on the throne, even if they were disobedient. How did God keep this promise?

  If you are in a group, read and discuss Psalm 89 together.

- What point was illustrated by the discussion of Egyptian pharaohs and the Ptolemies?

  If you are in a group, discuss the revolutionary truth that we have a King who truly is God, yet we can enter into His presence and speak directly to Him.

- Why does it not matter whether the witch of En-dor actually called up the spirit of Samuel?

  If you are in a group, discuss in what ways the abominable practices of divination and sorcery still exist in modern culture.

PRAYER

Commit to prayer what you have learned from God's Word in this lesson.

- Praise God that Christ is the fulfillment of the perfect Prophet, Priest, King, and Judge.
- Confess any times you may have practiced unbiblical spiritual practices.
- Thank God for the leaders He has chosen in your church, community, and nation.
- Ask God for wisdom as you apply the Old Testament principles from this lesson to your life.

REVIEW QUIZ

Use these multiple-choice questions to measure what you learned from this lesson.

1. What was the ultimate goal for establishing a system of appeals to priests and judges in Jerusalem?
   a. To uphold Mosaic law
   b. To oversee local judges
   c. To issue punishments
   d. To bring about peace

2. What was God's attitude toward having kings over Israel?
    a. He forbade it.
    b. He permitted it.
    c. He commanded it.
    d. He discouraged it.

3. What is the significance of stating that a king should not have many horses?
    a. Pagan kings competed on the basis of number of horses owned.
    b. Horses represented an overly militarized focus.
    c. Horses were designated as unclean by Mosaic law.
    d. Kings were not to have things that the people didn't have.

4. Why shouldn't a king have many wives?
    a. Many wives would complicate matters of heredity and succession.
    b. None of the Israelites were allowed multiple wives.
    c. They often bring with them foreign religions.
    d. They distract the king from affairs of state.

5. God commanded that the king of the Israelites should not be rich.
    a. True
    b. False

6. What sin did Saul fall into that is addressed in Deuteronomy 18?
    a. Eating meat that had been sacrificed
    b. Marrying foreign wives
    c. Erecting an Asherah pole
    d. Seeking to communicate with the dead

Answer Key—Laws about Leadership

REFLECTION & DISCUSSION QUESTIONS

Before the Video

What Do You Think?

> *These are personal questions. The answers should be based on your own knowledge and experience.*

Scripture Reading

- What did the Lord require of kings of Israel?

  The Lord would choose the king. The king was to make a copy of the book of the law and have it approved by the priests. He was to keep the book with him and read it every day so he would learn to fear the Lord, keep the law, and obey the Lord.

During the Video

Fulfillment in Jesus

- How do the laws in Deuteronomy 17 differ from those in Deuteronomy 16, which were the focus of the previous lesson?

  Deuteronomy 16 dealt with local leadership, in which judges could settle most issues. Deuteronomy 17 deals with more centralized leadership in Jerusalem, where Israelites can appeal to judges and priests.

- What roles outlined in Deuteronomy 17 are ultimately fulfilled in Jesus?

  Jesus is the ultimate Prophet, Priest, King, and Judge. God will accomplish His purposes through earthly kings, even as they anticipate the eternal King, Jesus. He is the great Prophet who speaks to God face-to-face. He is the great Priest and righteous Judge. The earthly prophets, priests, kings, and judges of Israel all pointed to Jesus.

Kings & Priests

- What were God's laws regarding kings?

  God's laws regarding kings in Israel were that they could not be foreigners; they had to avoid excesses, such as having many horses; they could not have many wives; they could not have excessive gold and silver; they had to love and obey God's law.

- What were God's laws regarding priests?

  God's laws regarding priests in Israel were that only the Levites were to serve as priests; they could not own a portion of the land but had to be supported by the people; they were to know the law of God and ensure that it is enforced.

After the Video

- In Psalm 89, God promised David that his sons would always sit on the throne, even if they were disobedient. How did God keep this promise?

  Israel would not always have an earthly king, as they were carried into exile. However, God's promise pointed to Jesus, the great King, the Son of David, who will rule forever.

- What point was illustrated by the discussion of Egyptian pharaohs and the Ptolemies?

  The king of Egypt was completely separate from the people and seen as a god. This continued even through three centuries of Ptolemies, who did not even have to learn to speak Egyptian. In contrast, God wanted the king of the Israelites to be part of the community and to relate to the people. Ultimately, He gives us a King who has faced temptations as we have and to whom we can speak directly.

- Why does it not matter whether or not the witch of En-dor actually called up the spirit of Samuel?

  God forbade as an abominable practice the use of mediums to commune with the spirits of the dead. He didn't say whether they were frauds or whether the practice was a real but dangerous power. He simply commanded against it, and Saul disobeyed.

REVIEW QUIZ

Lesson 12

1. **D.**

   While there were likely elements of all four options, the ultimate goal of the appeals system was to help ensure peace among the brothers and sisters of Israel.

2. **B.**

   God did not initially establish kings in Israel but knew that the people would come to want to be like other nations. He permitted it, and even outlined laws for it, but He did not command it.

3. **B.**

   Horses represented military strength. The Lord didn't want the Israelites to be overly militarized or to depend on their own strength in battle. He wanted them to trust in Him rather than in their military strength.

4. **C.**

   Many wives came through efforts to make political alliances, which meant they were foreigners. God repeatedly warned the Israelites to be careful of the influences of foreigners when it came to idolatry.

5. **A.**

   Depending on your interpretation of "excessive silver and gold" (Deut. 17:17), God didn't want kings to become too rich. Instead, He wanted them to be able to relate even to the average Israelite in the community.

6. **D.**

   Saul sought out the witch of En-dor in a seemingly successful attempt to communicate with the dead Samuel. God forbade this as an abominable practice in Deuteronomy 18.

13

Laws about Priests

INTRODUCTION

Deuteronomy 18–19 may seem to be a disparate collection of laws, warnings, and prophecies. In this lesson, Dr. Godfrey works through these passages to make sense of them, showing how they are unified and point forward to Jesus, the Messiah who fulfills Old Testament promises.

LEARNING GOALS

When you have finished this lesson, you should be able to:

- Understand God's requirement for us to be blameless
- Know God's guidelines for discerning true and false prophets
- Know that Jesus fulfills Old Testament promises

KEY IDEAS

- God's laws against pagan practices are to instruct us to worship Him in truth.
- Being blameless before God means not perfection but loyal commitment to Him.
- Jesus is the awaited Messiah who, like Moses, has a uniquely close relationship with God but who exceeds Moses as the second person of the Trinity.

REFLECTION & DISCUSSION QUESTIONS

Before the Video

What Do You Think?

Take a moment to answer the following questions. They will prepare you for the lecture.

- Imagine someone asks you, "In what ways does the Old Testament talk about Jesus?" How would you answer them?

- Are there modern-day false prophets? How can you tell?

Scripture Reading

I will raise up for them a prophet like you from among their brothers. And I will put my words in his mouth, and he shall speak to them all that I command him.

—Deuteronomy 18:18

- How would you respond to the view that Jesus was a prophet but not the Messiah?

During the Video

Answer the following questions while you watch the video. They will guide you through the lecture.

Deuteronomy 18:9–14   *0:00–14:13*

- How did David exemplify being "blameless," as Christians are called to be?

- What is the role of a prophet? What are the marks of a true prophet?

Deuteronomy 18:15–22   *14:13–25:54*

- What are the two interpretations of Moses' words "a prophet like me"?

- In what ways does Jesus fulfill the role of the coming Prophet?

After the Video

Answer the following questions after you have finished the lecture. They will help you identify and summarize the major points.

- According to this lesson, why are some people tempted to seek fortune tellers, palm readers, and even astrology predictions?

If you are in a group, discuss how you would dissuade a skeptic from consulting a fortune teller and instead point them to the Bible.

- How is discerning true and false prophets a "Protestant principle"?

  If you are in a group, discuss the circumstances that lead people to blindly follow a leader.

- How do you or your church practically love your neighbors by seeking justice, maintaining purity, and showing kindness?

  If you are in a group, discuss ways to practically love your neighbor without compromising the gospel.

PRAYER

Commit to prayer what you have learned from God's Word in this lesson.

- Praise God for sending a Prophet who fulfills and exceeds all expectations.
- Confess any times you have failed to love your neighbor.
- Thank God for the foundation of the Old Testament that sheds light on the New Testament.
- Ask God to help you practically love your neighbor.

REVIEW QUIZ

Use these multiple-choice questions to measure what you learned from this lesson.

1. The warnings in Deuteronomy 18 are, at their core, issues of worship and of truth.
   a. True
   b. False

2. According to this lesson, what is the meaning of "blameless" in Deuteronomy 18:13: "You shall be blameless before the LORD your God"?
   a. Above reproach
   b. Forgiven
   c. Sinless
   d. Loyal

3. Whose responsibility was it to discern true and false prophets?
   a. Kings
   b. Judges
   c. Levites
   d. Ordinary people

4. What did other prophets lack that kept them from being a prophet like Moses?
   a. Being chosen by God
   b. Performing miracles
   c. The Spirit and wisdom from God
   d. Complete intimacy with God

5. According to Dr. Godfrey, what theme underlies the Old Testament?
   a. God's Word is fulfilled.
   b. This is all temporary.
   c. The world is imperfect.
   d. God will return.

6. Which of these was *not* mentioned in the lecture as a ways to love one's neighbor in Deuteronomy?
   a. Serving others
   b. Seeking justice
   c. Maintaining purity
   d. Showing kindness

Answer Key—Laws about Priests

REFLECTION & DISCUSSION QUESTIONS

Before the Video

What Do You Think?

> *These are personal questions. The answers should be based on your own knowledge and experience.*

Scripture Reading

- How do you respond to the view that Jesus was a prophet but not the Messiah?

    Islam and other religions hold that Jesus was a prophet but not the Messiah or the promised Prophet. The New Testament teaches that Jesus is fully God, fully man, the Messiah, and the promised Prophet (Acts 3:22–26). We know Jesus is the Messiah because God has revealed it in the Bible.

During the Video

Deuteronomy 18:9–14

- How did David exemplify being "blameless," as Christians are called to be?

    David was certainly imperfect, and He even refused to repent for a time. However, David never utterly rejected the covenant of God. He remained a man after God's own heart. In time, the Spirit brought David to repentance and renewed faith. He remained loyal to God and faithful to His covenant.

- What is the role of a prophet? What are the marks of a true prophet?

    The role of a prophet is not to predict the future for people's material gain. Instead, prophets help people know God, know His will, and serve Him according to His truth. One mark of a true prophet is that what he says comes true. Another indicator is that the true prophet will not lead the people away from God.

Deuteronomy 18:15–22

- What are the two interpretations of Moses' words "a prophet like me"?

    In one sense, Moses was saying that he had been raised up by God as a prophet and that God would continue to raise up prophets through the whole history of Israel. In another sense, Moses was a prophet who spoke to the Lord face-to-face. Other prophets would not be like him in that sense until the Messiah.

- In what ways does Jesus fulfill the role of the coming Prophet?

    Peter, Stephen, and the author of Hebrews refer to Jesus as the Prophet who is greater than Moses. As the second person of the Trinity, Jesus has complete _intimacy with God, and in His earthly ministry, Jesus performed miracles that had never been seen before._

After the Video

- According to this lesson, why are some people tempted to seek fortune tellers, palm readers, and even astrology predictions?

  These avenues to knowing the future are about seeking truth or knowledge. Knowing the future is the first step in trying to control the future, which helps alleviate our fears about it. However, God says that we are to find truth in Him alone and in His Word.

- How is discerning true and false prophets a "Protestant principle"?

  We have a responsibility to honor those in authority over us. At the same time, we are to realize that our leaders are not infallible. The Bible teaches that there were good kings and bad kings. People have to be discerning and not just follow their leaders blindly. This is a Protestant principle, because in the Roman Catholic Church, the pope is seen as infallible when he speaks authoritatively on matters of theology and morality.

- How do you or your church practically love your neighbors by seeking justice, maintaining purity, and showing kindness?

  This is a personal question. It should be based on your own knowledge and experience. It should also include the ministry of deacons who are called by God to serve local congregation by leading in mercy ministry.

REVIEW QUIZ

Lesson 13

1. **A.**
   Deuteronomy 18 warns against child sacrifice and is, at its heart, about how the Israelites are to worship God. The other warning is about false teachers who claim to divine the future, which is about people's effort to seek truth.

2. **D.**
   Using the example of David, Dr. Godfrey teaches that being blameless does not mean being without sin. Instead, it means being completely committed and faithful to God's covenant.

3. **D.**
   The people, and not just their leaders, have to discern true and false prophets. Dr. Godfrey calls this a "Protestant principle" in that the need to make such discenments proves that leaders are not infallible even though we have the responsiblity to honor those in authority.

4. **D.**

   Moses had complete, face-to-face intimacy with God, which set him apart from other prophets. Many other prophets were chosen by God, were filled with God's Spirit and wisdom, and performed miracles. But until Jesus, no prophet had such intimacy with God as Moses.

5. **B.**

   Dr. Godfrey explains that underlying the Old Testament is a sense that this is all temporary. It is not permanent but will be fulfilled in the future. The Old Testament looks forward to the coming Prophet, Jesus.

6. **A.**

   While serving others is certainly a way to love one's neighbors and can even serve as a larger category for the other options for this question, it is not mentioned as a way to love neighbors described in Deuteronomy.

14

Laws about Loving Your Neighbor

INTRODUCTION

Jesus said that all the Law and the Prophets depend on the commands to love God and neighbor. In this lesson, Dr. Godfrey looks at God's laws about loving one's neighbor as they relate to crimes and warfare. Deuteronomy 19–20 addresses serious topics that any nation faces—issues of crime, punishment, and judgment.

LEARNING GOALS

When you have finished this lesson, you should be able to:

- Understand how God's laws promote love for one's neighbor
- Demonstrate how God's laws and the severity of punishment are meant to promote kindness between people

KEY IDEAS

- God established laws to protect against revenge killing, property encroachment, and false testimony.
- In times of war, God's laws preserve love for neighbors.
- God's judgment is real, just, and unavoidable.

REFLECTION & DISCUSSION QUESTIONS

Before the Video

What Do You Think?

Take a moment to answer the following questions. They will prepare you for the lecture.

- Is "eye for an eye" punishment fair?

- What do you think about rules for warfare?

Scripture Reading

*When you go out to war against your enemies, and see horses and chariots and an army larger than your own, you shall not be afraid of them, for the L*ORD *your God is with you, who brought you up out of the land of Egypt. And when you draw near to the battle, the priest shall come forward and speak to the people and shall say to them, "Hear, O Israel, today you are drawing near for battle against your enemies: let not your heart faint. Do not fear or panic or be in dread of them, for the L*ORD *your God is he who goes with you to fight for you against your enemies, to give you the victory."*

—Deuteronomy 20:1–4

- How did the Lord give Israelite soldiers courage?

During the Video

Answer the following questions while you watch the video. They will guide you through the lecture.

Laws Regarding Brothers   *0:00–13:58*

- How did cities of refuge support the practice of loving one's neighbor?

- What other laws in this section deal with kindness and justice regarding neighbors?

Laws Regarding Enemies   *13:58–26:11*

- What are some of God's laws regarding war?

- How do Old Testament laws about war relate to God's judgment?

After the Video

Answer the following questions after you have finished the lecture. They will help you identify and summarize the major points.

- How does studying these Old Testament laws help us better understand the suffering and death of Jesus?

If you are in a group, have the members discuss what might happen if a church does not emphasize a biblical understanding of God's laws. How will that church misinterpret other key Christian doctrines?

• Why does God allow His people to go to war?

If you are in a group, discuss modern warfare in light of Christian belief.

• Consider the discussion of God's judgment in this lesson. When is being nice actually doing harm to a neighbor?

If you are in a group, discuss how you might respond to a skeptic who says, "Jesus taught that people are to be nice to everyone and never to judge other people."

PRAYER

Commit to prayer what you have learned from God's Word in this lesson.

• Praise God for provisions of kindness even in the hardest situations.
• Confess any times you've been dishonest in being a witness for a neighbor.
• Thank God for those who go to war for just purposes.
• Ask God for opportunities to share your faith with your neighbors.

REVIEW QUIZ

Use these multiple-choice questions to measure what you learned from this lesson.

1. Cities of refuge were established for the protection of which group?
   a. Women whose husbands would not issue a divorce contract
   b. Foreigners who did not want to adopt Israelite customs
   c. Israelites who had accidentally committed murder
   d. Israelites who returned from foreign lands

2. Which law, discussed in this lesson, shows that God wants to ensure His people's portion in the land?
   a. A law that divides the land equally among the tribes
   b. A law that ensures land is passed down through the male line
   c. A law against moving a boundary marker
   d. A law against selling land to foreigners

3. Someone found to be a false witness was to be punished by exile from the land.
   a. True
   b. False

4. According to the law in Deuteronomy, which of these excused a person from war?
   a. Building a new house
   b. Being engaged to be married
   c. Being afraid of going to war
   d. All of the above

5. What is God's command regarding the people in a besieged city that is within the promised land?
   a. Kill everyone.
   b. If they resist you, kill the men.
   c. If they surrender, enslave them.
   d. If they submit to God, let them live.

6. Which of these laws about warfare shows God's compassion?
   a. Do not kill the livestock.
   b. Do not cut down the trees.
   c. Take the plunder for yourselves.
   d. You may build siege works.

Answer Key—
Laws about Loving Your Neighbor

REFLECTION & DISCUSSION QUESTIONS

Before the Video

What Do You Think?

> *These are personal questions. The answers should be based on your own knowledge and experience.*

Scripture Reading

- How does the Lord give Israelite soldiers courage?

  In this passage, God promises to be with them. He reminds them of His faithfulness in bringing them out of Egypt. He commands the priests to remind them of this.

During the Video

Laws Regarding Brothers

- How did cities of refuge support the practice of loving one's neighbor?

  Cities of refuge provided a place for people to flee who had committed an accidental murder. There, they were given protection from retribution by the murdered person's family. The accused would have to face justice, but he would be protected from a vengeance killing.

- What other laws in this section deal with kindness and justice regarding neighbors?

  This section includes a law about not moving a neighbor's boundary stone. Other laws deal with witnesses. They command that witnesses give honest testimony, that more than one witness be required, and that a false witness shall receive "eye for an eye" punishment.

Laws Regarding Enemies

- What are some of God's laws regarding war?

  God told the Israelites not to be afraid. Before going into battle, a priest was to come forward and remind them of God's strength and faithfulness. Several types of people were allowed to go home from war—those who were building a home or planting a vineyard, those who were engaged, and those who were afraid. God gave commands regarding besieged cities based on their distance and their response. God commanded the Israelites not to cut down the trees in a besieged city.

- How do Old Testament laws about war relate to God's judgment?

  In the Old Testament, God allowed war as a form of His judgment against pagan nations. The laws allowed the Israelites to kill everyone in cities in the promised land. These laws serve as a reminder that God's judgment is real and terrible, so we do not love our neighbors well if we shelter them from the knowledge of God's coming judgment.

After the Video

- How does studying these Old Testament laws help us better understand the suffering and death of Jesus?

  Jesus was betrayed by false witnesses. According to the law, these witnesses should have received the punishment they sought for Jesus. Instead, He suffered and died. The false witnesses betrayed not only God but also their neighbor.

- Why does God allow His people to go to war?

  God allows the Israelites to go to war as judgment against the nations that do not love and obey God. The reason God called the Israelites to go to war against the peoples in the promised land was for the purpose of Israel's purity, because these peoples would have led Israel into idolatry.

- Consider the discussion of God's judgment in this lesson. When is "being nice" actually doing harm to a neighbor?

  The example given in this lesson is perpetuating the attitude that "if we all just agree that there is no hell, it will go away." God's judgment is real, and there's nothing nice about letting others live in ignorance of that fact. Loving one's neighbors means bringing them closer to God, the ultimate kindness.

REVIEW QUIZ

Lesson 14

1. **C.**

   Cities of refuge were established to protect Israelites who had accidentally committed murder. There, they could face justice while also being protected from a vengeance killing.

2. **C.**

   This lesson addressed the law in Deuteronomy 19:14: "You shall not move your neighbor's landmark, which the men of old have set, in the inheritance that you will hold in the land that the Lord your God is giving you to possess."

3. **B.**

   Deuteronomy 19:18–19 states, "If the witness is a false witness and has accused his brother falsely, then you shall do to him as he had meant to do to his brother."

4. **D.**

   Deuteronomy 20 lists all of these, in addition to planting a new vineyard, as legitimate reasons to be excused from fighting.

5. **A.**

   God commanded that everyone in a besieged city that is within the land of promise must be killed. This was an effort to wipe out idolatry and keep the Israelites pure.

6. **B.**

   God forbade the Israelites from cutting down food-bearing trees as a way of ensuring that life can go on.

15

Laws about Conflict

INTRODUCTION

In this lesson, by examining Deuteronomy 20–21, Dr. Godfrey provides cultural and contextual understanding for several laws that may seem unrelated or not make sense to a modern reader. He then builds a bridge from the Old Testament to the New Testament to show how understanding these laws sheds light on the life and death of Jesus Christ.

LEARNING GOALS

When you have finished this lesson, you should be able to:

- Know God's various laws that address relational conflict
- Relate Old Testament law to the accusation, betrayal, and death of Jesus
- See the importance of laws concerning purity

KEY IDEAS

- God's laws, even in seemingly obscure situations, promote purity, kindness, and justice.
- Jesus' accusation, betrayal, and death held special symbolic meaning for Jews familiar with Old Testament law.

REFLECTION & DISCUSSION QUESTIONS

Before the Video

What Do You Think?

Take a moment to answer the following questions. They will prepare you for the lecture.

- Why is it important to study Old Testament law?

- What aspects of the Old Testament are most helpful to you in understanding and appreciating the person and work of Christ?

Scripture Reading

If a man has two wives, the one loved and the other unloved, and both the loved and the unloved have borne him children, and if the firstborn son belongs to the unloved, then on the day when he assigns his possessions as an inheritance to his sons, he may not treat the son of the loved as the firstborn in preference to the son of the unloved, who is the firstborn, but he shall acknowledge the firstborn, the son of the unloved, by giving him a double portion of all that he has, for he is the firstfruits of his strength. The right of the firstborn is his.

—Deuteronomy 21:15–17

- How does the Lord view the firstborn, based on this passage?

During the Video

Answer the following questions while you watch the video. They will guide you through the lecture.

Deuteronomy 21:1–17   *0:00–12:15*

- How do the laws discussed in this section relate to the themes of purity, kindness, and justice?

- What is the significance of the discussion of firstborn and firstfruits?

Deuteronomy 21:18–22:4   *12:15–25:39*

- What is the significance of Jesus' being accused in Matthew 11 of "eating and drinking"?

- In what ways do we see the Old Testament foreshadowing the person and work of Jesus?

After the Video

Answer the following questions after you have finished the lecture. They will help you identify and summarize the major points.

- What command did God make regarding divorcing a wife who was a captive of war? What does this reveal about God?

If you are in a group, discuss how an understanding of the background of Old Testament law helps reveal both the mercy and the justice of God, especially as that mercy and justice are expressed in difficult social situations.

- What is the significance of the commands regarding a man hanged on a tree in Deuteronomy 21:22–23?

If you are in a group, look up and discuss the passages mentioned in this section of the lesson: Acts 5:30; Acts 10:39; Galatians 3:13; 1 Peter 2:24. Based on these readings, discuss Luke's, Paul's, and Peter's views of the Old Testament and how they relate to Jesus.

- How does Dr. Godfrey define purity at the end of this lesson?

If you are in a group, discuss how this definition applies to contemporary Christian living.

PRAYER

Commit to prayer what you have learned from God's Word in this lesson.

- Praise God for the righteousness that comes by faith and not through the law.
- Confess how you may have overlooked some or all of the Old Testament as a means to understanding Jesus.
- Thank God for an ever-growing understanding and appreciation of Jesus.
- Ask God to continue to help you love your neighbor.

REVIEW QUIZ

Use these multiple-choice questions to measure what you learned from this lesson.

1. If an Israelite comes across a dead body, he is to call a priest and offer a sacrifice.
   a. True
   b. False

2. Which of these is *not* a requirement for marrying a woman taken captive in war?
   a. Shaving her hair
   b. Cutting her nails
   c. Offering a sacrifice
   d. Allowing her to mourn

3. According to Deuteronomy, what is the prescribed punishment for a rebellious son who is brought before the elders?
   a. Flogging him with a rod
   b. Sending him into exile
   c. Revoking his inheritance
   d. Stoning him to death

4. According to this lesson, the man hanged on a tree in Deuteronomy 21 can be compared to whom?
   a. Rebellious sons
   b. Drunkards
   c. Judas
   d. Jesus

5. What chapter heading is given to the first section of Deuteronomy 22 in some Bibles?
   a. Laws about Purity
   b. Showing Love for Life
   c. Laws on Cleanliness
   d. Various Laws

6. What was an Israelite required to do if he found a wandering animal?
   a. Allow it to go free
   b. Bring it before the assembly
   c. Care for it until it is returned to its owner
   d. Offer it as a sacrifice to the Lord

Answer Key—Laws about Conflict

REFLECTION & DISCUSSION QUESTIONS

Before the Video

What Do You Think?

> *These are personal questions. The answers should be based on your own knowledge and experience.*

Scripture Reading

- How does the Lord view the firstborn, based on this passage?

> *The Lord regards the firstborn as entitled to the firstfruits of his father, no matter how loved or unloved his mother is. In addition, the firstborn should inherit a double portion.*

During the Video

Deuteronomy 21:1–17

- How do the laws discussed in this section relate to the themes of purity, kindness, and justice?

> *The laws about how to treat a dead body relate to purity. The sacrifice that is commanded is to preserve purity in the land. The laws about how to treat women captured during war have to do with kindness. They are about treating women kindly compared to the standard of the day. The laws about the rights of the firstborn relate to justice.*

- What is the significance of the discussion of firstborn and firstfruits?

> *Deuteronomy establishes laws for the inheritance of the firstborn son, who is to receive a double portion, which relates to God's broader saving purpose. Israel is the firstborn son of God, God is to receive the firstfruits of the crops and the flocks, and even the king of Israel is the firstfruit of God's purpose. Dr. Godfrey explains the many ways in which Jesus is the firstborn and how we, as Christians, are the firstfruits of the Spirit.*

Deuteronomy 21:18–22:4

- What is the significance of Jesus' being accused in Matthew 11 of "eating and drinking"?

> *"Eating and drinking" evokes gluttony and drunkenness. These are the sins that are given in Deuteronomy 21 as signs of a rebellious son. Since the punishment for a rebellious son was stoning to death, the charges against Jesus were equivalent to a call for His death.*

- In what ways do we see the Old Testament foreshadowing the person and work of Jesus?

  Understanding the Old Testament helps us better understand Jesus' roles as Priest, Prophet, Judge, King, Shepherd, and promised Messiah. In this section of Deuteronomy alone, we better understand the significance of Jesus as firstborn, deserving of God's firstfruits, yet accused and betrayed as a rebellious son and hanged on a tree as a curse.

After the Video

- What command did God make regarding divorcing a wife who was a captive of war? What does this reveal about God?

  In Deuteronomy 21:10–14, God allowed Israelites to divorce a wife who had been taken captive in war. However, once divorced, she could not be returned to slavery or be sold. She was to be treated like any other Israelite. This reveals the kindness and mercy of God even as it is woven into Israel's policies on war, foreigners, and marriages that ends in divorce.

- What is the significance of the commands regarding a man hanged on a tree in Deuteronomy 21:22–23?

  Hanging on a tree was a sign of being cursed and abandoned. It served as a reminder to others that the dead person was a sinner. This discussion reminds us that Jesus was rejected and abandoned. He became a curse for us that we might be freed from the curse.

- How does Dr. Godfrey define purity at the end of this lesson?

  Dr. Godfrey defines purity as a kind of love and caring. Sometimes purity is defined as keeping separate those things that should not be mixed.

REVIEW QUIZ

Lesson 15

1. **A.**
   Deuteronomy 21:1–9 explains the law regarding the victim of an unsolved murder. It involves summoning priests and offering sacrifice over the dead.

2. **C.**
   Deuteronomy 21:10–14 describes the steps to be taken by an Israelite who wanted to marry a captive of war. The commands include shaving her head, cutting her nails, removing her clothing, and allowing her to mourn the loss of her people. The commands do not mention anything about offering a sacrifice.

3. **D.**

   Although there seems to be no record of this ever actually happening, Deuteronomy 21:18–21 commands that the parents of a rebellious son to take him to the city gates, summon the elders, and stone him to death.

4. **D.**

   Dr. Godfrey highlights this law about a man hanged from a tree to help us see Jesus and appreciate His sacrifice.

5. **D.**

   The section is usually called "Various Laws" or "Miscellaneous Laws." Although this might seem to be a random collection of laws, they all related to upholding the purity of one's neighbor.

6. **C.**

   Deuteronomy 22:1–4 required the Israelites to seek out the owner of the lost animal and, if unable to find the owner, to care for the animal until his brother came looking for it. In this way, they would show love for their neighbors.

16

Laws Relating to Purity

INTRODUCTION

In this lesson, Dr. Godfrey continues to examine laws about loving one's neighbor. In the first half of Deuteronomy 22, we'll see how these laws have deeper meanings that relate to God's desire that His people remain pure. In the second half, we'll examine laws regarding sexual purity and maintaining purity in the assembly.

LEARNING GOALS

When you have finished this lesson, you should be able to:

- Explain the deeper meaning behind the purity laws in Deuteronomy 22
- Understand the importance of sexual purity
- Know God's laws about purity in the assembly

KEY IDEAS

- God wants His people to maintain purity in their lives and in their relationships.
- One way to maintain purity is to avoid mixing things that shouldn't be mixed.
- Purity should also be maintained in sexual relationships.

REFLECTION & DISCUSSION QUESTIONS

Before the Video

What Do You Think?

Take a moment to answer the following questions. They will prepare you for the lecture.

- What does *purity* mean?

- Are sexual immorality and sexual temptation similar today to Old Testament times or different?

Scripture Reading

Now as the church submits to Christ, so also wives should submit in everything to their husbands. Husbands, love your wives, as Christ loved the church and gave himself up for her, that he might sanctify her, having cleansed her by the washing of water with the word, so that he might present the church to himself in splendor, without spot or wrinkle or any such thing, that she might be holy and without blemish.

—Ephesians 5:24–27

• How does this passage elevate the importance of sexual purity in marriage?

During the Video

Answer the following questions while you watch the video. They will guide you through the lecture.

Various Laws   *0:00–12:32*

• Note the various laws mentioned in this section and what each one reveals about God.

Sexual Immorality   *12:32–25:45*

• How does Deuteronomy establish fair treatment of women in a time when that wasn't the norm?

• Why do laws about sexual purity focus so much on the external and not the internal?

• How do laws about entering the assembly relate to sexual purity?

After the Video

Answer the following questions after you have finished the lecture. They will help you identify and summarize the major points.

• What message does Deuteronomy have for Christians in its discussion of male and female garments?

If you are in a group, discuss how Deuteronomy 22 relates to broader social movements that try to eliminate fixed distinctions between men and women, and what our calling to love our neighbor requires.

- What is the significance of the command not to wear cloth of wool and linen mixed together?

If you are in a group, discuss the significance of God's laws that relate to clothing. How should God's laws about clothing in the Old Testament influence the decisions that Christians make about what they wear?

- Why were people excluded from the assembly of Israel for being impure?

If you are in a group, discuss how a Christian should pursue purity but also take the gospel to those who are not Christians.

PRAYER

Commit to prayer what you have learned from God's Word in this lesson.

- Praise God for the blood of Jesus that makes us pure.
- Confess instances of impurity of heart when confronted with temptation.
- Thank God for His salvation that is received by faith and not on the basis of our works.
- Ask God to help you live up to His standard of purity.

REVIEW QUIZ

Use these multiple-choice questions to measure what you learned from this lesson.

1. Which of these is a general theme among many of the laws in Deuteronomy 22?
   a. How obeying God will allow you to prosper
   b. How laws apply differently to men and to women
   c. Not mixing things that shouldn't be mixed
   d. Maintaining sexual purity as an inward sign of devotion to God

2. Which of these is reminiscent of the command not to kill a mother bird if you find a nest?
   a. The command to care for an animal until its owner can claim it
   b. The commandment to honor your father and mother
   c. Jesus' words that not a single sparrow falls apart from God's knowing
   d. The story of how Moses' mother saved him from death

3. Which of these commands likely has a purpose beyond what is just practical?
   a. Wear tassels on your garment.
   b. Build a parapet on your roof.
   c. Don't sow two different kinds of seed.
   d. Don't plow with an ox and a donkey.

4. According to the lecture, what principle is at the center of the chiasm on loving one's neighbor?
   a. Entering the tabernacle
   b. Laws about clothing
   c. Cleanliness
   d. Sexual purity

5. According to a law in Deuteronomy 22, a woman who is raped in the countryside is never to be punished.
   a. True
   b. False

6. Which of these is *not* excluded from the assembly?
   a. A man whose testicles are crushed
   b. A person born of a forbidden union
   c. An Egyptian
   d. A Moabite

Answer Key—Laws Relating to Purity

REFLECTION & DISCUSSION QUESTIONS

Before the Video

What Do You Think?

> *These are personal questions. The answers should be based on your own knowledge and experience.*

Scripture Reading

- How does this passage elevate the importance of sexual purity in marriage?

> *This passage establishes marriage as a model of the relationship between Christ and the church. Doing so places a significant call on husbands and wives to be loving and pure.*

During the Video

Various Laws

- Note the various laws mentioned in this section and what each one reveals in a bigger sense about God.

> *The command about men not wearing a woman's cloak and vice versa reveals that God values the gender identities He created. The command about letting the mother bird live reveals that God values life and that we should, too. The command about building a parapet shows that God wants us to value our neighbor's life. Commands about sowing seeds and plowing are probably practical. The command about wool and linen garments shows that God wants the sacred to be kept separate from the ordinary. The command to wear tassels on the garment reveals that God wants to be continually remembered and obeyed.*

Sexual Immorality

- How does Deuteronomy establish fair treatment of women in a time when that wasn't the norm?

> *In cases of adultery, men and women faced equally harsh punishment. In the case of rape, a woman who called out was not punished, but the perpetrator was. If the rape occurred in the country, it was assumed that the woman had no one to call out to, so she was considered innocent.*

- Why do laws about sexual purity focus so much on the external and not the internal?

> *Internal feelings are not denied or seen as insignificant. However, the focus of the*

laws about sexual purity is on Israel's calling to exemplify to the world a separate, pure life. In that pursuit, it is the external that is the focus.

- How do laws about entering the assembly relate to sexual purity?

  Some of the exclusions are based on people born of forbidden marriages. God established laws to maintain purity in the tabernacle, and some of those laws relate to purity in marriage and the birth of children.

After the Video

- What modern-day message does Deuteronomy have for Christians in its discussion of male and female garments?

  Deuteronomy commands that a male is not to wear a woman's cloak and vice versa, as it is an abomination to God. The broader lesson is one of gender identity. God created mankind male and female, and this command upholds the idea that the two should remain distinct. These laws mean that there shouldn't be any attempt to blur this distinction.

- What is the significance of the command not to wear cloth of wool and linen mixed together?

  Exodus explains that the curtains of the tabernacle and the priestly garments were to be made of wool and linen woven together. Avoiding this material in everyday garments shows that the holy is separate from the ordinary and that people shouldn't presume to be holy by wearing such material.

- Why were people excluded from the assembly of Israel for being impure?

  People were excluded from the assembly, based on their own impurity or that of their ancestors, to maintain the relationship with God and His people. Israel was called to be holy, and the holiness required for God's presence in the tabernacle extended beyond the tabernacle to the outer courts and throughout the camp of Israel.

REVIEW QUIZ

Lesson 16

1. **C.**

   Most of the laws in Deuteronomy 22:5–12 have to do with the theme of not mixing things that shouldn't be mixed. These include garments for men and women, sowing different kinds of seeds in a field, and plowing with two different kinds of animals. The next section of Deuteronomy 22 does deal with sexual immorality, but Dr. Godfrey shows that the emphasis is on external signs of obedience.

2. **B.**

   This command is reminiscent of the fifth commandment because both include the provision "that it may go well with you, and that you may live long." It speaks of God's regard for life, as the mother bird will be able to go on and lay more eggs.

3. **A.**

   As explained in the book of Numbers, wearing tassels on one's garment was to remind the wearer of God's commands and to provide a reminder to obey them. They didn't serve any practical purpose, but they served a spiritual one. The other commands listed seem to have a practical aim, such as preventing injury.

4. **D.**

   Dr. Godfrey identifies sexual purity as the center of the chiasm on loving one's neighbor. When it came to purity, sexual purity was particularly important to the Israelites.

5. **A.**

   The woman was given the benefit of the doubt that she called out but there was no one to hear her. Only the perpetrator was punished in that situation.

6. **C.**

   Deuteronomy 23:7–8 explains that Egyptians after the third generation should not be excluded from the assembly. All of the others listed are never to be allowed into the assembly.

17

What Loving Your Neighbor Looks Like

INTRODUCTION

Concluding the section on loving your neighbor, Dr. Godfrey explores Deuteronomy 23–25. This lesson will show the importance and meaning of various laws in these chapters as Dr. Godfrey guides us through a close look at God's justice for the nation of Israel against its enemies.

LEARNING GOALS

When you have finished this lesson, you should be able to:

- Explain the deeper meaning behind the laws in Deuteronomy 23–25
- Apply God's Old Testament laws to modern situations
- Understand the role of the Amalekites in the history of Israel

KEY IDEAS

- God established laws for the treatment of brothers, the needy, and enemies.
- God's justice has a wider purpose than students of the Bible might first think.

REFLECTION & DISCUSSION QUESTIONS

Before the Video

What Do You Think?

Take a moment to answer the following questions. They will prepare you for the lecture.

- These lessons show that God cares about the seemingly insignificant parts of the lives of His people. How does this truth inform Christian discipleship?

- How do churches in your community work together?

Scripture Reading

When you reap your harvest in your field and forget a sheaf in the field, you shall not go back to get it. It shall be for the sojourner, the fatherless, and the widow, that the LORD your God may bless you in all the work of your hands. When you beat your olive trees, you shall not go over them again. It shall be for the sojourner, the fatherless, and the widow. When you gather the grapes of your vineyard, you shall not strip it afterward. It shall be for the sojourner, the fatherless, and the widow. You shall remember that you were a slave in the land of Egypt; therefore I command you to do this.

—Deuteronomy 24:19–22

- What is the purpose of and reasoning behind these commands?

During the Video

Answer the following questions while you watch the video. They will guide you through the lecture.

Loving Your Neighbor   *0:00–13:52*

- What was the unfortunate historical outcome of God's command not to charge a brother interest?

- What provision does God make for loving a neighbor who is hungry?

The Amalekites   *13:52–24:27*

- What did the Amalekites do wrong, and what is God's judgment against them?

- How did Saul disobey God, and what was the outcome of his disobedience?

After the Video

Answer the following questions after you have finished the lecture. They will help you identify and summarize the major points.

- How did the poor and hungry in Old Testament times differ from the poor and hungry today?

If you are in a group, discuss how churches can help the poor in their communities and around the world.

- Dr. Godfrey suggests that churches with greater resources could partner with churches with fewer resources. What are other ways that churches could share resources to accomplish God's mission for the church?

If you are in a group, have the members discuss their role in funding the church and her mission through tithing and Christian generosity.

- How does David's ultimate defeat of the Amalekites point to Christ?

If you are in a group, discuss the balance between wanting to see the enemies of the church saved and wanting to see the enemies of the church receive God's justice.

PRAYER

Commit to prayer what you have learned from God's Word in this lesson.

- Praise God for His definitive triumph over the enemies of sin and death.
- Confess any patterns in your life of willful disobedience to God.
- Thank God for your pastor, elders, deacons, and church staff.
- Ask God to bring unity to churches in your community.

REVIEW QUIZ

Use these multiple-choice questions to measure what you learned from this lesson.

1. What is the restriction placed on charging interest in Deuteronomy 23:19?
   a. You may not charge interest to foreigners.
   b. You may not charge interest to your brother.
   c. You may not charge interest on money that is lent.
   d. You may not charge interest on food that is lent.

2. What important shift in understanding Deuteronomy did John Calvin promote?
   a. Christians who gain profit from charging interest should give it all to the church.
   b. Christians and Jews are allowed to prepare food on the Sabbath.
   c. Christians are allowed to charge other Christians interest.
   d. Christian pastors should be paid out of the church collection.

3. What complaint did the Pharisees have against Jesus and His disciples for their taking grain from another's field?
   a. They did not pay for it.
   b. They put some in their bags.
   c. They used their hands to thresh it.
   d. They did so on the Sabbath.

4. Paul twice quotes "You shall not muzzle an ox when it is treading out the grain" to argue that pastors ought to be paid.
   a. True
   b. False

5. What did Moses do in response to the attack by the Amalekites?
   a. He assigned a rearguard.
   b. He had their king executed.
   c. He held up his arms and prayed.
   d. He led the Israelites along a different route.

6. How did the Amalekites continue to become a snare to the people of God?
   a. They aided Israel's enemies.
   b. They fought the Israelites.
   c. They took Israelites' wives.
   d. All of the above

Answer Key—
What Loving Your Neighbor Looks Like

REFLECTION & DISCUSSION QUESTIONS

Before the Video

What Do You Think?

> *These are personal questions. The answers should be based on your own knowledge and experience.*

Scripture Reading

- What is the purpose of and reasoning behind these commands?

> *The purpose of these commands is to provide food for the needy. The reasoning behind it is that the Israelites should remember that they were once slaves in Egypt. They once had nothing, and everything they now have is from God.*

During the Video

Loving Your Neighbor

- What was the unfortunate historical outcome of God's command not to charge a brother interest?

> *The church in the Middle Ages interpreted this verse to apply only to those in the church. That excluded Jews, allowing the Jews to charge Christians interest but not allowing Christians to charge other Christians interest. The Christians grew to resent this, which fed anti-Semitism.*

- What provision does God make for loving a neighbor who is hungry?

> *Deuteronomy 23:24–25 allows for Israelites to take grapes or grain to eat from another's field. It does not, however, allow them to fill a bag or use tools to harvest.*

The Amalekites

- What did the Amalekites do wrong, and what was God's judgment against them?

> *When the Israelites came out of Egypt, they were faint, weary, hungry, and thirsty. That's when Amalek attacked them. Not only that, but the Amalekites did not attack bravely from the front. Instead, they picked off the Israelites who were lagging behind. Therefore, the Lord commanded that the Israelites wipe them out completely.*

- How did Saul disobey God, and what was the outcome of his disobedience?

  Instead of killing the Amalekites and blotting them out from the earth, Saul spared King Agag. As a result, the Amalekites killed Saul in battle and continued to be a snare to the Israelites.

After the Video

- How did the poor and hungry in Old Testament times differ from the poor and hungry today?

  In Old Testament times, the poor and hungry lived near farms so they could glean the leftover grain. Today, many of the poor live in cities, where they have better access to public services.

- Dr. Godfrey suggests that churches with greater resources could partner with churches with fewer resources. What are other ways that churches could share resources to accomplish God's mission for the church?

  This is a personal question. The answer should be based on your own knowledge, experience, and ideas about the mission of the church.

- How does David's ultimate defeat of the Amalekites point to Christ?

  David put a final end to the Amalekites who had for so long been a snare to the Israelites, and he gave rewards to his soldiers. Similarly, Christ's triumph over the enemies of sin and death is complete, and He rewards those who follow Him.

REVIEW QUIZ

Lesson 17

1. **B.**
   The restriction is on charging interest on anything that is lent (money, food, etc.) to a fellow Israelite. However, the Israelites were allowed to charge interest to foreigners.

2. **C.**
   John Calvin interpreted Deuteronomy 23:19 to apply only to Jews living in the promised land. Although Roman Catholics at the time disagreed, Calvin taught that all Christians can charge interest.

3. **D.**
   Deuteronomy 23:25 allows Israelites to take grain from another's field to eat if they are hungry. It does prohibit filling one's bag, but Jesus and His disciples didn't do that. The Pharisees complained because they picked the grain on the Sabbath. Threshing grain with one's hands was not against the law, but doing so on the Sabbath was considered work.

4. **A.**

   While this verse can be interpreted to promote kindness to animals in the context of Deuteronomy, Paul uses it to argue that pastors must be paid. He looks at the greater principle behind the command, which is that workers should be compensated.

5. **C.**

   The battle against the Amalekites, described in Exodus 17, is when Moses prayed and held up his hands to bring Israel the victory. When he grew tired, Aaron and Hur supported him.

6. **D.**

   The Amalekites continued to be a snare to the Israelites in all of the ways listed. They aided the Moabites and the Midianites in battles against Israel. They directly fought the Israelites and killed Saul. They took some of David's wives and the wives of other Israelites.

18

Warnings That Protect Us

INTRODUCTION

Deuteronomy 26–27 moves us back into the subject of warnings. Dr. Godfrey explains how these warnings are actually an expression of God's love and care for His people. Warnings about the past help forge an identity, and warnings about the future set God's people on the right path.

LEARNING GOALS

When you have finished this lesson, you should be able to:

- Understand how identity is rooted in and remembered through history
- Understand the two-sided nature of our loving relationship with God
- Know the warnings God gave as the Israelites entered the promised land

KEY IDEAS

- Remembering the past helps us understand who we are today.
- Our relationship with God is a balance of faith and obedience.
- God reminds His people again and again how to obey Him.

REFLECTION & DISCUSSION QUESTIONS

Before the Video

What Do You Think?

Take a moment to answer the following questions. They will prepare you for the lecture.

- What are major events in your life that have helped shape who you are today?

- What warnings do people give to their children or friends out of love and concern for them?

Scripture Reading

*This day the L*ORD *your God commands you to do these statutes and rules. You shall therefore be careful to do them with all your heart and with all your soul. You have declared today that the L*ORD *is your God, and that you will walk in his ways, and keep his statutes and his commandments and his rules, and will obey his voice. And the L*ORD *has declared today that you are a people for his treasured possession, as he has promised you, and that you are to keep all his commandments, and that he will set you in praise and in fame and in honor high above all nations that he has made, and that you shall be a people holy to the L*ORD *your God, as he promised.*

—Deuteronomy 26:16–19

- Who is involved in this agreement, and what are the stipulations and blessings?

During the Video

Answer the following questions while you watch the video. They will guide you through the lecture.

Remembering   *0:00–9:58*

- What are the many benefits of bringing firstfruits to the Lord during the Feast of Weeks?

- How is Jewish history Christian history?

Loving   *9:58–25:46*

- Describe the two-sided nature of the relationship with God addressed in this lesson.

- How do God's warnings in the form of twelve curses reflect the Ten Commandments?

After the Video

Answer the following questions after you have finished the lecture. They will help you identify and summarize the major points.

- How did the Israelites' history help establish their identity?

If you are in a group, discuss how the three main parts of a Christian's conversion story—life before conversion, conversion, and life after conversion—shape the Christian's identity.

- How is American identity different from the national identity of other nations?

If you are in a group, discuss the aspects of your nation's history that you feel are important to your national identity.

- What is the significance of God's command to the Israelites to set up stones when they crossed the Jordan?

If you are in a group, discuss any markers in your life that serve as a reminder and testimony of what God has done for you.

PRAYER

Commit to prayer what you have learned from God's Word in this lesson.

- Praise God for always keeping His promises even when we fail to keep ours.
- Confess any reluctance that you have to obey God despite His faithfulness.
- Thank God for warnings that keep us from danger and bring us closer to Him.
- Ask God to help you balance your understanding of justification and sanctification.

REVIEW QUIZ

Use these multiple-choice questions to measure what you learned from this lesson.

1. Which act, described in Deuteronomy 26, is associated with the Feast of Weeks?
   a. Building small booths
   b. Giving money to the poor
   c. Making atonement for sin
   d. Bringing firstfruits to Jerusalem

2. Which quote illustrates Martin Luther's view of the importance of history?
   a. "History is written by the victors."
   b. "Historians are the greatest of men."
   c. "We are not makers of history. We are made by history."
   d. "Those who don't know history are destined to repeat it."

3. What warning from earlier in Deuteronomy is repeated in Deuteronomy 26:16?
   a. You shall not
   b. Be careful
   c. Lest you shall die
   d. Seek not

4. To what does Dr. Godfrey compare God's loving call and our loving response?
   a. Passing from earthly life to eternal life
   b. The prayer of salvation
   c. Infant baptism
   d. The marriage ceremony

5. God commanded one tribe onto Mount Ebal to set the blessing and eleven tribes onto Mount Gerizim to set the curse.
   a. True
   b. False

6. What is significant about the curses spoken on the mountain?
   a. There are twelve of them, just as there are twelve tribes.
   b. They are spoken by Dan, the most rebellious of the tribes.
   c. They correspond to all ten of the Ten Commandments.
   d. They each correspond to a related blessing.

Answer Key—Warnings That Protect Us

REFLECTION & DISCUSSION QUESTIONS

Before the Video

What Do You Think?

> *These are personal questions. The answers should be based on your own knowledge and experience.*

Scripture Reading

- Who is involved in this agreement, and what are the stipulations and blessings?

> *The agreement is between God and His covenant people, who will continue to sin and are called to obedience. The commitment of God's people is to follow all of God's laws and keep all His commands, which they will never do perfectly. God's promise is to make His people His treasured possession and to set them in praise and fame and in honor high above all the nations. God is faithful and always keeps His promises.*

During the Video

Remembering

- What are the many benefits of bringing firstfruits to the Lord during the Feast of Weeks?

> *Bringing firstfruits during the Feast of Weeks supported the temple and the priesthood. It also created fellowship among everyone coming together in Jerusalem and reinforced the identity of the Israelites by reminding them of their history.*

- How is Jewish history Christian history?

> *The history of the Israelites is Christian history. God has torn down the wall of division between Jews and gentiles, bringing the gentiles into the covenants of Israel. Because of Jesus, gentiles are included in God's covenants with Israel. Remembering the history of the Israelites' rescue from slavery also reminds Christians that we were brought out of slavery to sin by Jesus.*

Loving

- Describe the two-sided nature of the relationship with God addressed in this lesson.

> *For our part, a relationship with God is not to be simply an external adherence to laws but an engagement of the heart. Christians are to obey God with all their heart and soul. God has called us to both justification and sanctification. On the opposite*

side of the relationship, we are God's treasured possession, loved and cared for by Him. He has promised to set us on high as His honored people before the world.

- How do God's warnings in the form of twelve curses reflect the Ten Commandments?

  The first curse about making images corresponds to the second commandment. The second curse about honoring parents corresponds to the fifth commandment. The third curse about moving a landmark corresponds to the eighth commandment. The fourth curse about misleading a blind man corresponds to the ninth commandment. The fifth curse about perverting justice could correspond to the tenth, eighth, or ninth commandment. Curses six through nine about sexual sins correspond to the seventh commandment. Curses ten and eleven about murder correspond to the sixth commandment. The twelfth curse is a summary.

After the Video

- How did the Israelites' history help establish their identity?

  God constantly reminded the Israelites of their history as a means of establishing their identity. They were a people chosen by God and set apart for His glory. They were slaves in Egypt, but He brought them out to the land of promise. This act of rescue and faithfulness established a basis for their trust in and commitment to God.

- How is American identity different from the national identity of other nations?

  Dr. Godfrey observes that the United States does not have an ethnic identity like many other nations have. Whether a person's American heritage goes back many generations or they are a brand-new citizen, he or she is considered American. The aspects of a shared history bind people of different ethnic backgrounds.

- What is the significance of God's command to the Israelites to set up stones when they crossed the Jordan?

  The stones were an outward expression of the reality of God's covenant and His warning. The stones were to carry the words of Deuteronomy, which show that the Israelites came this far not by their own strength but by God's blessing. The stones were a reminder that they were God's covenant people.

REVIEW QUIZ

Lesson 18

1. **D.**

   Deuteronomy 26 begins with a description of the Feast of Weeks, in which Israelites brought the firstfruits to Jerusalem. Although the chapter gets into the concept of the tithe, it is not a monetary donation to the poor but the produce that is given to the Levites.

2. **B.**

   Martin Luther said: "Historians are the greatest of men. We cannot praise them too much." Studying and teaching history is important for national and spiritual identity.

3. **B.**

   Deuteronomy 26:16 says: "This day the LORD your God commands you to do these statutes and rules. You shall therefore be careful to do them with all your heart and with all your soul." The warning to be careful is repeated several times in Deuteronomy 5–10.

4. **C.**

   Dr. Godfrey shared a portion of the baptismal form of the Dutch Reformed Church of the sixteenth century. It contains one part about God's character, love, and action and then another part about our response in loving, trusting, and cleaving to Him.

5. **B.**

   The tribes were divided equally between the two peaks, with six tribes on each. Mount Gerizim represented the blessing and Mount Ebal represented the curse.

6. **A.**

   There were twelve curses spoken, just as there were twelve tribes of Israel. This may signify that the curses can apply to any and all of the tribes. Although there is some overall correlation to the Ten Commandments, the curses do not cover all ten.

19

Warnings That Call Us to Faithfulness

INTRODUCTION

In keeping with the theme of caution, Deuteronomy 28 focuses on blessings and curses. In this lecture, Dr. Godfrey will examine what these blessings and curses meant for Israel, what they mean for Christians, and how they hold significance for our eternal future.

LEARNING GOALS

When you have finished this lesson, you should be able to:

- Understand the relationship between obedience and faith
- Know God's promises for those who obey and His curses for those who don't
- See how God's blessings and curses serve as prophecy for the Israelites and for Christians

KEY IDEAS

- God commands obedience as an outgrowth of faith in Him.
- God promises to abundantly bless all areas of life for those who obey Him.
- God's blessings for this life point forward to the holiness of the new heavens and new earth.

REFLECTION & DISCUSSION QUESTIONS

Before the Video

What Do You Think?

Take a moment to answer the following questions. They will prepare you for the lecture.

- As you think about God's blessings, do you mainly think about blessings in this life or blessings experienced only in the life to come? Why?

- What happens, spiritually, when you disobey God?

Scripture Reading

And if you faithfully obey the voice of the Lord your God, being careful to do all his commandments that I command you today, the Lord your God will set you high above all the nations of the earth. And all these blessings shall come upon you and overtake you, if you obey the voice of the Lord your God.

—Deuteronomy 28:1–2

- For whom is this blessing intended, and when?

During the Video

Answer the following questions while you watch the video. They will guide you through the lecture.

Blessings   *0:00–9:54*

- What is the relationship between obedience and faith?

- What is God's "land promise" for believers, and how does it relate to Deuteronomy?

Curses   *9:54–24:53*

- How does the section on God's curses parallel the section on blessings?

- When do God's warnings become prophecy? Why is this significant for the moment that Moses delivered this sermon?

After the Video

Answer the following questions after you have finished the lecture. They will help you identify and summarize the major points.

- How do God's blessings and curses as described in Deuteronomy 28 relate to the past, present, and future?

  If you are in a group, list as many blessings as you can think of that Christians experience. Which blessings are Christians prone to focus on, and which are they prone to miss? Why?

- What is the importance of serving God in attitude and not just in action?

  If you are in a group, discuss ways to cultivate a thankful and joyful attitude toward God regardless of how or where you are serving Him.

- How can tragedy and hardship function in a believer's life to drive him closer to God?

  If you are in a group, discuss how you could support and encourage someone whose faith is shaken by tragedy or hardship.

PRAYER

Commit to prayer what you have learned from God's Word in this lesson.

- Praise God for His promise of a new heaven and a new earth.
- Confess any times you've served merely out of obligation rather than joy.
- Thank God for the many blessings in your present life.
- Ask God to help you remain faithful to Him.

REVIEW QUIZ

Use these multiple-choice questions to measure what you learned from this lesson.

1. The Westminster Confession of Faith states, "The Mosaic economy is an administration of the covenant of grace with a legal character to it."
   a. True
   b. False

2. Deuteronomy 28 relates the theme "Be careful" to which of these?
   a. Teaching children
   b. Recording God's laws
   c. Blessings and curses
   d. History and future

3. Where is the focus of covenant keeping always found?
   a. In the law
   b. At the temple
   c. In observing festivals
   d. In worship

4. What is a specific curse described in Deuteronomy 28 as discussed in the lecture?
   a. The ark of the covenant will fall into the hands of Israel's enemies.
   b. Israel will become a byword or a proverb representing destruction.
   c. The nations will lend to Israel but not borrow from them.
   d. Israel will lose all record of the law of the Lord.

5. How do God's curses recall the Israelites' history in Egypt?
   a. God will cause a famine to wipe out the Israelites.
   b. God will drown the Israelites in the Red Sea.
   c. God will strike the Israelites with boils and tumors.
   d. God will strike down the firstborn sons of the Israelites.

6. What analogy is used in the lecture to apply God's warnings to churches today?
   a. The lampstand in the heavenly temple
   b. The faithfulness of the early church in Acts
   c. The global influence of today's church
   d. The ownership of land by the Vatican

Answer Key—
Warnings That Call Us to Faithfulness

Before the Video

What Do You Think?

> *These are personal questions. The answers should be based on your own knowledge and experience.*

Scripture Reading

- For whom is this blessing intended, and when?

  At the time this blessing was spoken, it was for the Israelites as they entered the promised land. However, as the lecture will reveal, it has significance for Christians and for our future.

During the Video

Blessings

- What is the relationship between obedience and faith?

  The Bible teaches a balance of both obedience and faith. Obedience is not a means by which we earn God's blessing; rather, it is the effect and evidence of faith. To receive God's blessing, we must live out the grace He has worked in us.

- What is God's "land promise" for believers, and how does it relate to Deuteronomy?

  God's promise to restore Israel to the land is ultimately fulfilled in the new heavens and new earth where righteousness dwells. In Deuteronomy, the promised land of the old covenant points forward to the holiness of the new heavens and new earth that Christians will experience after Christ returns in glory. In Deuteronomy, God promises blessings on all areas of life to those who obey His commands, which again points forward to the fullness of God's blessing that is to come.

Curses

- How does the section on God's curses parallel the section on blessings?

  Both the blessings and the curses relate to all areas of life—work, family, fields, politics. Both take time to realize, even though the curses were said to be done quickly. In addition, both blessings and curses point to a future in which these will be absolute.

- When do God's warnings become prophecy? Why is this significant for the moment that Moses delivered this sermon?

  In Deuteronomy 28:36, God's curses shift from warnings to prophecy. At this point, the curse includes mention of the exile of Israel, the curse of losing their promised land. It is significant for the moment Moses delivered this sermon because they were just about to enter the land God promised to them.

After the Video

- How do God's blessings and curses as described in Deuteronomy 28 relate to the past, present, and future?

  As we read Deuteronomy, we can see how God's blessings and curses played out in the history of the Israelites. In the present, God's blessings and curses relate to our earthly lives. In a future sense, the blessings and curses point forward to the new heavens and new earth.

- What is the importance of serving God in attitude and not just in action?

  Deuteronomy 28:47 describes a curse that results not from a failure to serve God but a failure to serve Him with joyfulness and gladness of heart. It shows that God is not just keeping a tally of our actions but seeks the transformation of our hearts. He wants us to love Him and love others the way He loves us, with joy and gladness.

- How can tragedy and hardship function in a believer's life to drive him closer to God?

  Tragedy and hardship can serve to draw a believer closer to God, remind the believer that this world is still subject to the fall, help the believer search out and repent of remaining sin, encourage the believer to look to God alone for hope and life, and teach the believer to long for the blessing of the new heavens and new earth.

REVIEW QUIZ

Lesson 19

1. **A.**

   The Westminster Confession of Faith and Dr. Godfrey in this lesson teach that the Mosaic law involves a balance of obedience and faith, of works and grace.

2. **C.**

   Deuteronomy 28 is broken into two main sections, one on blessings and one on curses. In each, the theme of "Be careful" is present. Be careful to obey God so you receive His blessings, and be careful not to disobey God or you will experience curses.

3. **D.**

   Although the law, the temple, and the festivals all relate in some way to covenant keeping, the focus is always found in worship. Deuteronomy begins with and repeats here the importance of worship as a way of faithfully looking directly to God.

4. **B.**

   The list of curses in Deuteronomy 28 is extensive and devastating, but the specific one mentioned in this lesson has to do with Israel's becoming a byword or a proverb. It warns that Israel could become so utterly destroyed as to serve only as a warning or "horror" to other nations.

5. **C.**

   Deuteronomy 28:27 says that the Lord will strike the Israelites "with the boils of Egypt, and with tumors and scabs and itch, of which you cannot be healed." It is a warning to be careful lest God inflict the same afflictions He did on the Egyptians.

6. **A.**

   In this lesson, Dr. Godfrey looks to Revelation, in which Christ walks in the heavenly temple among the lampstands. God is warning Christians that congregations can lose their faith and be removed as lampstands from the heavenly temple, just as Israel lost faith and was exiled from the promised land.

20

Warnings That Call Us to Obedience

INTRODUCTION

In this lesson, Dr. Godfrey will shed light on theologically difficult verses and concepts in Deuteronomy 29–30 as we learn about the individual's responsibility to be obedient, the interpretation of prophecy concerning Israel, and the roles of faith and obedience in the life of the believer. By looking at the New Testament to help interpret Deuteronomy, we will come to a deeper understanding of God's provision for righteousness.

LEARNING GOALS

When you have finished this lesson, you should be able to:

- Apply to modern Christian living God's call on the Israelites for obedience
- Interpret Deuteronomy in light of New Testament teaching
- Further your understanding of the roles of faith and obedience

KEY IDEAS

- We are responsible for our own sin and our own obedience, though we can rely on God to change our hearts.
- Moses taught that righteousness comes through faith, and faith leads to obedience.
- A lack of obedience leads to a life of sin, but overemphasis on obedience neglects the role of faith.
- Paul and Moses agreed on and both taught the same fundamental principles of righteousness.

REFLECTION & DISCUSSION QUESTIONS

Before the Video

What Do You Think?

Take a moment to answer the following questions. They will prepare you for the lecture.

- How do you balance the idea of personal responsibility with the knowledge that God chooses, changes, and enlightens His people?

- How do you relate Old Testament law to New Testament grace?

Scripture Reading

*I call heaven and earth to witness against you today, that I have set before you life and death, blessing and curse. Therefore choose life, that you and your offspring may live, loving the L*ORD *your God, obeying his voice and holding fast to him, for he is your life and length of days.*

—Deuteronomy 30:19–20a

- What does it mean to choose life?

During the Video

Answer the following questions while you watch the video. They will guide you through the lecture.

Our Responsibility   *0:00–9:10*

- What should be the response to the possibility that God has not given some "a heart to understand or eyes to see or ears to hear"?

- What is "covenant faithfulness" as defined in this part of the lesson?

Deuteronomy & Romans   *9:10–25:25*

- How could you interpret Deuteronomy 30 in light of Romans 10?

- According to Paul, how did the Israelites misinterpret the law?

After the Video

Answer the following questions after you have finished the lecture. They will help you identify and summarize the major points.

- How does Dr. Godfrey explain the seeming contradiction between the command to "circumcise your own heart" and the statement that "God will circumcise your heart"?

If you are in a group, discuss what internal and external evidence a Christian should look for in his life as a sign that God has changed his heart.

- What lessons can individuals and churches today learn from the Israelites?

If you are in a group, discuss whether Christians today should study more or less of the history of Israel. Why or why not?

- How do the Old and New Testaments work hand in hand on issues discussed in this lesson?

If you are in a group, discuss any misconceptions that have been cleared up for you as you study Deuteronomy.

PRAYER

Commit to prayer what you have learned from God's Word in this lesson.

- Praise God for His ability to change hearts.
- Confess any times you've sought righteousness through works and obedience.
- Thank God for sending a Savior to save you and free you from your sin.
- Ask God to help you understand what He has revealed to you and to help you trust Him in areas that remain hidden.

REVIEW QUIZ

Use these multiple-choice questions to measure what you learned from this lesson.

1. What is the "root bearing poisonous and bitter fruit" described in Deuteronomy 29?
   a. A person whose greed keeps him from obeying laws about giving
   b. A false teacher who draws the Israelites toward idolatry
   c. One who lets rebellion against God grow in his heart
   d. An enemy who attacks when Israel is most vulnerable

2. What does Deuteronomy 29:29 say belongs to the Lord?
    a. Plans for the future
    b. The secret things
    c. Knowledge of good and evil
    d. Wisdom and power

3. According to this lesson, what elements are present in the verse, "And when all these things come upon you, the blessing and the curse, which I have set before you"?
    a. Life and death
    b. Past and future
    c. Possibility and prophecy
    d. Give and take

4. In Deuteronomy 30, Moses taught the Israelites to exercise their free will to merit salvation.
    a. True
    b. False

5. With which of these principles would Moses disagree?
    a. We are saved by faith.
    b. Faith leads to obedience.
    c. The law shows us we are sinful.
    d. Obedience leads to righteousness.

6. What is the relationship between the law and the promise as explained in Galatians?
    a. The promise came first, and the law supports it.
    b. The law came first, and the promise supports it.
    c. The promise and the law both bring righteousness.
    d. The promise does away with the law.

Answer Key—
Warnings That Call Us to Obedience

REFLECTION & DISCUSSION QUESTIONS

Before the Video

What Do You Think?

> *These are personal questions. The answers should be based on your own knowledge and experience.*

Scripture Reading

- What does it mean to choose life?

> *In this passage is explained as "loving the LORD your God, obeying his voice and holding fast to him." Choosing life means loving the Lord, which is characterized by our commitment to Him and our obedience to His voice. This is the path that leads to blessing and life for us and our children.*

During the Video

Our Responsibility

- What should be the response to the possibility that God has not given some "a heart to understand or eyes to see or ears to hear"?

> *There's a delicate interplay between God's purpose and our responsibility. Whether or not God blesses us with a heart to be obedient, He has called us to faithfulness and obedience. We are responsible for our own sins, even though it is God who sanctifies us and enables us to resist sin and temptation.*

- What is "covenant faithfulness" as defined in this part of the lesson?

> *This part of the lecture discusses covenant faithfulness as a commitment to God. Despite not knowing the future or understanding all aspects of God's plan, we are commanded to be faithful to God, to worship Him alone, and to be devoted to Him. We are to rely on our knowledge of what God has revealed and the history of His faithfulness.*

Deuteronomy & Romans

- How could you interpret Deuteronomy 30 in light of Romans 10?

> *Deuteronomy 30:11–20 tells the Israelites that God's commandment was not far from the Israelites and that His Word was in their heart and in their mouth to do it, so God set before them a choice between life and death. Paul quotes a portion of*

this text in Romans 10:6, calling it a "righteousness based on faith." Some appeal to Paul's statement in Romans 10:5 to say that Moses only understood the law in terms of works, but Paul argues the law was never intended to be pursued as if it could be achieved by works.

- According to Paul, how did the Israelites misinterpret the law?

  Paul's argument in Romans 9:30–32 was that the Israelites pursued the law that would lead to righteousness, and they did not pursue it by faith. God had given them a covenant of grace, mercy, and faith that leads to obedience, but they turned it into a covenant of merit and works. Instead of relying on the law to reveal sinfulness and the need for a Savior, Israel attempted to save themselves by their own righteousness under the law.

After the Video

- How does Dr. Godfrey explain the seeming contradiction between the command to "circumcise your own heart" and the statement that "God will circumcise your heart"?

  In Deuteronomy 30:6, God promised to change the hearts of the Israelites. However, this didn't relieve the Israelites of responsibility to circumcise their own hearts as commanded in Deuteronomy 10:16. They were called to be faithful and obey, yet that ultimately happened as the Lord changed their hearts.

- What lessons can individuals and churches today learn from the Israelites?

  Israel's main mistakes were complete disobedience and abandonment of the law at one end of the spectrum and abuse of the law in seeking righteousness at the other end. Similarly, individuals and churches today can fall into these two extremes of disobedience and self-righteousness. The lesson to be learned is to look to the law to teach us to recognize sin and our need for a Savior but to look to Jesus for righteousness.

- How do the Old and New Testament work hand in hand on issues discussed in this lesson?

  By interpreting Deuteronomy and Romans together, we learn that the Old and New Testaments have the same fundamental teachings. The law shows us our sinfulness and need for a Savior. We are called to faith and obedience, but we cannot achieve righteousness through our own efforts. Faith is the instrument by which God declares us righteous and leads us to obey.

REVIEW QUIZ

Lesson 20

1. **C.**

   The "root bearing poisonous and bitter fruit" is the person who lets rebellion against God grow in his heart. It's the one who assures himself that he is safe, though he is walking in stubbornness. This rebellion may lead to greed, disobedience, and even false teaching, but the root is rebellion against God.

2. **B.**

   Deuteronomy 29:29 says, "The secret things belong to the LORD our God, but the things that are revealed belong to us and to our children forever, that we may do all the words of this law."

3. **C.**

   Dr. Godfrey discussed this verse, which serves as an example of how possibility runs into prophecy. God is predicting that the possibilities of blessings and curses will come to pass as Israel moves into the promised land and then into exile.

4. **B.**

   Moses' call to the Israelites to choose life is not something that can be used as an Arminian proof text or as grounds for the belief that Moses thought the law was solely of works. It is a misconception to believe that the law was only based on an economy of works devoid of faith, though Israel pursued the law as such, which is what Paul addresses in Romans.

5. **D.**

   According to the lecture, interpreting Deuteronomy and Romans together shows that Moses taught, "We are saved by faith, which leads to love, which leads to obedience, which leads us to see that we're still a sinful people and that we need a Savior." Moses did not teach that righteousness comes through obedience but that it comes through faith.

6. **A.**

   The covenant with Abraham came 430 years before the law was given to Moses. Therefore, the covenant comes first, and the law supports it. Although Christ fulfills the law, that does not mean it is abolished completely as a moral guide. Furthermore, Deuteronomy and Romans both teach that righteousness comes through faith, not through the law.

21

Deuteronomy Points Us to Christ

INTRODUCTION

To conclude this study on Deuteronomy, Dr. Godfrey teaches through the beauty of its final chapters, in which Moses transitions leadership to Joshua before he dies. Once again, we will see that the curses that would befall Israel because of the nation's disobedience are met by the blessings of a gracious God, showing us that, ultimately, Deuteronomy points us to Christ.

LEARNING GOALS

When you have finished this lesson, you should be able to:

- Understand how themes of sin and redemption run from the Old Testament through the New Testament
- Know the details surrounding Moses' transition of leadership and death
- Know the curses and the blessings that God pronounced on Israel and how they relate to Christians

KEY IDEAS

- Before his death, Moses sang a long song of curses and blessings on Israel.
- Despite disobedience, sin, and unfaithfulness of His people, God shows steadfast love.
- Deuteronomy paints the picture of a Great High Priest, King of kings, and righteous Israelite who would come to fulfill the law.

REFLECTION & DISCUSSION QUESTIONS

Before the Video

What Do You Think?

Take a moment to answer the following questions. They will prepare you for the lecture.

- In what areas of life do you see reflections of God's character as a loving, caring authority enforcing strict consequences?

- What have been the most meaningful themes to you in this series?

Scripture Reading

There is none like God, O Jeshurun, who rides through the heavens to your help through the skies in his majesty. The eternal God is your dwelling place, and underneath are the everlasting arms. And he thrust out the enemy before you and said, "Destroy." So Israel lived in safety, Jacob lived alone in a land of grain and wine, whose heavens drop down dew. Happy are you, O Israel! Who is like you, a people saved by the LORD, the shield of your help, and the sword of your triumph! Your enemies shall come fawning to you, and you shall tread upon their backs.

—Deuteronomy 33:26–29

- How does this passage apply to Christians?

During the Video

Answer the following questions while you watch the video. They will guide you through the lecture.

Looking to the Future   0:00–9:52

- What are some of the steps that take place in transitioning leadership from Moses to Joshua?

- How does Paul pick up on the theme of Moses' song?

Redemption   9:52–24:33

- What lessons can we learn from God's judgment on Moses in not allowing him to enter the promised land?

- How do the Lord's blessings, spoken to the tribes through Moses, echo earlier themes of Deuteronomy?

After the Video

Answer the following questions after you have finished the lecture. They will help you identify and summarize the major points.

- What are some of the positive and negative aspects of the Song of Moses?

If you are in a group, discuss the Song of Moses in Deuteronomy 32:1–43. What would the original audience of Moses' song have thought when they first heard it? What would they have felt?

- What is the picture of God that Moses paints at the end of his blessings in Deuteronomy 33?

If you are in a group, discuss how these traits show up elsewhere in the Bible.

- How does the book of Deuteronomy end by pointing us forward?

If you are in a group, discuss how your church might be different if more people in your church learned what you have learned about Deuteronomy.

PRAYER

Commit to prayer what you have learned from God's Word in this lesson.

- Praise God for His everlasting care and love for His people.
- Confess your self-dependence, that at times you don't realize your need for God.
- Thank God for what you've learned through this teaching series.
- Ask God to help you continue growing in knowledge of Him and faithfulness to Him.

REVIEW QUIZ

Use these multiple-choice questions to measure what you learned from this lesson.

1. What was to be done with the law that Moses wrote down?
    a. It was to be kept sealed inside the ark of the covenant.
    b. It was to be read aloud every seven years.
    c. It was to be copied and kept in every household.
    d. It was to be sent to all the nations.

2. What name did Moses use in his song to refer to Israel, perhaps ironically, to say they were rebellious?
   a. Hebrews
   b. Sons of Abraham
   c. Jeshurun
   d. Jews

3. Which of the following is the last action that Moses was allowed to take?
   a. Seeing the promised land
   b. Entering the promised land
   c. Living in the promised land
   d. Being buried in the promised land

4. The final words of Moses to the Israelites recorded in Deuteronomy 33 are words of blessing.
   a. True
   b. False

5. Which tribe does Moses say "is prince among his brothers. A firstborn bull—he has majesty, and his horns are the horns of a wild ox"?
   a. Judah
   b. Reuben
   c. Simeon
   d. Joseph

6. Which of these accurately describes the burial of Moses?
   a. He was laid to rest in the promised land.
   b. After centuries, his burial place was lost.
   c. The event was attended by all Israel.
   d. He was buried secretly.

Answer Key— Deuteronomy Points Us to Christ

REFLECTION & DISCUSSION QUESTIONS

Before the Video

What Do You Think?

> *These are personal questions. The answers should be based on your own knowledge and experience.*

Scripture Reading

- How does this passage apply to Christians?

  The character of God is unchanging—His help, comfort, protection, and provision still hold true. The concept of a sinful people redeemed by God's faithfulness is the hope of those who follow Jesus.

During the Video

Looking to the Future

- What are some of the steps that take place in transitioning leadership from Moses to Joshua?

  In transitioning the leadership of Israel from Moses to Joshua, the Lord told Joshua to be strong and courageous, and the Lord promised never to leave or forsake him. Moses also wrote down the law and put it in the ark of the covenant, and Joshua and Moses appeared at the tent of meeting so the Lord could publicly commission Joshua.

- How does Paul pick up on the theme of Moses' song?

  The theme of the Song of Moses is to tell how Israel forsook God. Paul continues this theme in Romans 11 when he says that the reason God includes gentiles in His covenant is to make Israel jealous. Both Moses and Paul address God's redemptive purposes.

Redemption

- What lessons can we learn from God's judgment on Moses in not allowing him to enter the promised land?

  Sin is serious, and God's judgment of sin is serious. However, God's judgment doesn't necessarily reflect the person's eternal destiny. We can learn from this instance that even Moses needs a Savior.

- How do the Lord's blessings, spoken to the tribes through Moses, echo earlier themes of Deuteronomy?

  The very presence of these blessings after a long song of cursing speaks to God's redemptive plans. The blessing on Levi reiterates the call to faithfulness, ministry, and service. Joseph, who was great in faithfulness, receives great blessings. The final general blessings remind Israel of God's commitment to their care and that He will not forsake them.

After the Video

- What are some of the positive and negative aspects of the Song of Moses?

  Some negative aspects are that the song witnesses against Israel because they are going to forsake the Lord; that it points out the people's sinfulness; and that the Lord becomes angry with Israel. Some positive aspects are that it is a reminder of Israel's history, covenant, character, and problems from which future generations can learn; that it has some gentle, encouraging dimensions to it; and that it highlights the Lord's care and provision.

- What is the picture of God that Moses paints at the end of his blessings in Deuteronomy 33?

  God is shown as being unlike any other, riding through the heavens to our help. He is shown as powerful against enemies but gentle to His people. He is protector and conqueror. His majesty, His faithfulness, and His everlasting love are all present in this description.

- How does the book of Deuteronomy end by pointing us forward?

  It reminds us that God will raise up another prophet even greater than Moses. It calls us to faith and love, but even more, it calls us to look for the One whom God would send to fulfill His promises. He would be the true Israelite who keeps the law completely for us and for our salvation.

REVIEW QUIZ

Lesson 21

1. **B.**
   The written law was to be read aloud every seven years at the Feast of Booths. It would be a reminder to the people of Israel to carefully follow its commands and learn to fear the Lord.

2. **C.**
   The name Jeshurun means "upright," but the song tells how Israel is not upright but "fat" in its indifference, rebellion, and idolatry.

3. **A.**
   God's judgment on Moses was that he was not allowed to enter the promised land. However, God allowed him to see the promised land from Mount Nebo before he died.

4. **A.**

   Deuteronomy 33 records a lengthy blessing that Moses spoke over the tribes of Israel just before his death.

5. **D.**

   Moses lavished this long blessing on the tribe of Joseph. Reuben and Judah both received very short blessings, and Simeon seems left out altogether, though he might be included with a blessing of one of his brothers.

6. **D.**

   Moses was buried in secret, probably to prevent him from being honored above God. John Calvin commented, "It is appropriate that great men be buried secretly so that their graves become not an object of pilgrimage."